D0457608

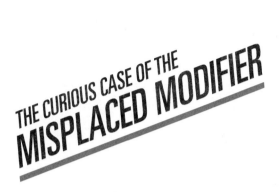

BONNIE TRENGA
THE CURIOUS CASE OF THE
MISPLACED MODIFIER
HOW TO SOLVE THE MYSTERIES OF WEAK WRITING

WRITER'S DIGEST BOOKS
Cincinnati, Ohio
www.writersdigest.com

10 09 08 07 06   5 4 3 2 1

Distributed in Canada by Fraser Direct, 100 Armstrong Avenue, Georgetown, ON, Canada L7G 5S4, Tel: (905) 877-4411. Distributed in the U.K. and Europe by David & Charles, Brunel House, Newton Abbot, Devon, TQ12 4PU, England, Tel: (+44) 1626 323200, Fax: (+44) 1626 323319, E-mail: mail@davidandcharles.co.uk. Distributed in Australia by Capricorn Link, P.O. Box 704, Windsor, NSW 2756 Australia, Tel: (02) 4577-3555.

Library of Congress Cataloging-in-Publication Data
Trenga, Bonnie.
 The curious case of the misplaced modifier : how to solve the seven mysteries of weak writing / by Bonnie Trenga.
      p. cm.
 Includes index.
 ISBN-13: 978-1-58297-389-0 (hardcover ; alk. paper)
 ISBN-10: 1-58297-389-X
1. English language--Sentences--Problems, exercises, etc. 2. English language--Rhetoric--Problems, exercises, etc. 3. Report writing--Problems, exercises, etc. I. Title.
 PE1441.T74 2006   2005037969
 808'.042--dc22

Edited by Jane Friedman
Designed by Grace Ring
Production coordinated by Robin Richie
Illustrations © Photodisc / Getty Images

F+W PUBLICATIONS, INC.

DEDICATION

for Jake and Natalie

TABLE OF CONTENTS

Introduction I

Chapter One: The Tantalizing Tale of Passive Voice 8
Chapter Two: The Illuminating Investigation
    Into the Nasty Nominalization 18
Chapter Three: The Peculiar Puzzle
    of the Vague *-ing* Word 28
Chapter Four: The Delicious Drama
    of the Weak Verb 38
Chapter Five: The Curious Case
    of the Misplaced Modifier 46
Chapter Six: The Confusing Caper
    Concerning the Super-Long Sentence 60
Chapter Seven: The Stretched-Out Story
    of the Wordy Writing 72

Appendix One: The Top Ten Writing Misdemeanors 89
Appendix Two: Answer Key 110
Appendix Three: Glossary 124
Appendix Four: Weak Writing Rap Sheet 132

Index 142

INTRODUCTION

How to write well might seem like a mystery to you. You wonder how your favorite writer succeeds in making you want to read more. Likewise, you're unsure exactly why a dull writer makes you want to shelve the book or ditch the magazine after just a paragraph. Writers you like probably use clear subjects, active verbs, and concise phrasing. They limit the length of their sentences and take advantage of colorful vocabulary. Chances are, writers you dislike bog you down with vague, wordy sentences that run too long. Or maybe they're too pompous. Even if their grammar and punctuation are correct, their writing can still be confusing or dry.

I've been a professional copyeditor and proofreader since 1996 and have continually corrected the same writing problems. No matter what my clients write—end-user computer books, advertising copy, annual reports, school essays, novels, magazine articles, you name it—both beginning and experienced writers make the same mistakes. Sometimes their grammar and punctuation are a bit off, but the main culprit is usually their sentence structure—the way they build their sentences.

After years of editing the same kinds of poor sentences over and over, I decided to write this book. At that time, none of the available books addressed the ubiquitous writing problems I kept fixing. Plenty of grammar-filled writing books lined the shelves, but I didn't think writers benefited much from wading through two hundred pages of dry rules and discussions of uncommon mistakes. I felt writers needed a non-grammar-focused guide that would help them improve their writing after just two or three chapters. So, this book covers the seven writing mistakes I encounter all the time. After you've gotten through the first few chapters, your writing will have improved immensely. When you've finished all of them, you'll be amazed at how clear your writing has become.

Writing books that are really grammar books might make you feel that your English teacher—the one with the tight bun, frumpy scowl, and inflexible red pen—is looking over your shoulder. In this book, we take a friendlier approach. I say *we* instead of *I* because I the author don't want to be *the know-it-all writing genius*. (I'm far from it!) I won't talk down to you or bore you. Rather, we'll work together to detect and correct poorly worded sentences.

Writing well takes more than getting your grammar right. Grammatically correct sentences can still be weak and unclear. So, instead of concentrating on grammar, we'll focus on building better sentences. We'll unravel the mystery of how to craft clear sentences that inform and perhaps entertain readers. We'll say au revoir to bulky, bland, and confusing writing. As you'll see, the difference between a page-turner and a book used as a doorstop is often in the writer's phrasing. Compare these sentences:

- The sentence was written by me.

- The writing of the sentence was done.

- Writing the sentence happened.

- I wrote a clear, easy-to-follow sentence—a sentence my audience actually enjoyed reading!

The first three examples sound rather vague and unpolished. Readers who encounter such sentences often don't know who or what the writer is talking about. The last sentence, on the other hand, is specific—we know who did what—and it has a bit of character.

Poor writing has many roots. To start with, we tend to write the way we speak. When we talk, our hand gestures and intonation help listeners understand our meaning, so it doesn't matter if we ramble on a bit. When we write, though, readers see just our words, so we need to state clearly what we're trying to get across. Readers don't want to work hard to figure it out.

We don't intend to baffle our readers, but sometimes we do because we don't know how to spot and correct lapses in clarity. Sometimes what's in our minds doesn't translate to the page. Other times we fall into bad habits, such as using vague phrasing or passive sentence structure. Whatever the reason, awkward phrasing and outright errors can damage a writer's credibility and make readers lose interest.

In this book, we'll use a very elementary technique to help us see writing problems more easily: We'll literally underline problem spots. Let's say we're focusing on eliminating weak verbs, as we do in chapter four. It may seem a bit mechanical to underline all the verbs. However, that's the only way to see if you've used *is*, *are*, *was*, and *were* too many times. At first, you'll have to go back to each underline and deal with the problem. After lots of practice, though, you'll be able to recognize writing weaknesses before they appear, and prevent them.

You can practice the underlining technique right here in this book. Every chapter begins with a mystery filled with the writing mistake we investigate in that chapter. After you've finished reviewing multiple examples of a particular writing problem, you'll get to correct each story. In addition, the book contains four useful appendices: The Top Ten Writing Misdemeanors, a look at some common writing mistakes; an answer key for the exercises; a glossary of terms;

and the Weak Writing Rap Sheet, which summarizes problem areas and solutions.

Don't be upset if you can't improve all aspects of your writing at once. This book covers a lot of material, so you won't be able to remember everything. As when you're learning to play a sport or an instrument, the more you practice, the better you'll become. To write well, you need to keep at it. Do the exercises in the book, refer to its chapters when you need to brush up, and practice on your own.

You can benefit from having a coach (besides me) to support you. Find yourself a writing buddy, an experienced writer who can read what you've written and provide useful criticism. Even without a writing coach, you can still improve by playing writing detective with yourself. Examine the evidence (look at your sentence structure), and then solve the crime (create a better sentence).

- -

As you work on improving your writing throughout this book, keep these tips in mind:

- Your first draft shouldn't be your final draft.

- It will be easier to rewrite if you set aside your first draft for a bit before revising it. Even if you have a close deadline, schedule a short interval between writing and rewriting.

- When you're writing a rough draft, don't worry about achieving instant perfection. Scribble now and shape later.

- Don't get too attached to any particular sentence. You can probably make it better.

- Be suspicious of yourself. You'll catch lots of mistakes if you reread your writing with a critical eye and assume it's imperfect.

- Having a problem? Just rewrite the sentence.

- Practice a lot. As you read a book or the newspaper, look for poorly written sentences and practice rewriting them. Poor writing and outright errors abound in the real world.

Chapter One

THE TANTALIZING TALE OF PASSIVE VOICE

Clues that you've used passive voice:

- a form of the verb *to be* (often *is*, *are*, *was*, or *were*)
- a past participle (a past-tense form of a verb: *convicted* or *stolen*)
- the word *by*

The pile of case files was carefully laid out as Detective Pinkersolve decided which one should be tackled first.

A puzzling caper at the local museum of modern art needed to be solved quickly, so the facts were examined by her. Last night, everything was being prepared for opening day of the much-anticipated exhibition of self-portraits. It was discovered by the cleaning crew that one painting had been defaced. When the crime scene was studied closely by the detective, it was revealed that a portrait of a man had been scribbled on with red crayon. It was decided a visit needed to be paid to the man whose self-portrait had been given a mustache.

When the artist was interviewed, it was noted that his scruffy red mustache was the same as the one depicted by the self-portrait. When confronted, the artist explained that his painting had not been ready at the deadline, so the museum had been snuck into and some last-minute touches added. Although an apology was issued and a fine paid, bad press could not be avoided. Artistic success was never achieved, so career options were evaluated. A few ideas were suggested and the case file closed.

Passive writing is vague, wordy writing that confuses or bores readers. It confuses them because they can't tell who is doing what; it bores them because they encounter verbs such as *was* and *were* over and over. Passive sentence structure—the topic of the first three chapters of this book—usually equals poor writing.

One of the most common vague writing styles is passive voice, which you may have heard of (but don't worry if you haven't). Passive voice is overused by writers and disliked by readers. (Sorry, let's rephrase that: Writers overuse passive voice, and readers dislike it.) This chapter shows you how to turn sentences filled with monotonous passive voice into easy-to-follow sentences that contain clearer subjects, stronger verbs, and fewer words.

HOW TO DETECT AND CORRECT PASSIVE VOICE

To understand passive voice, let's briefly discuss active voice, the clearest and most direct way to present your ideas. In an active sentence, the *subject* performs the action, and the *object* receives it.

Active
The sausage seller bit the hot dog vendor.

Here the sausage seller (the subject) is performing the action, and the hot dog vendor (the object) is receiving the action. However, if you turn the object of this sentence into the subject, you create passive voice.

Passive
The hot dog vendor <u>was bitten by</u> the sausage seller.

Watch out for the three clues that signal passive voice. Sometimes passive sentences contain only one or two of these elements; other times, all three appear.

1. A form of the verb *to be* (*am, is, are, was, were, be*).

2. A past participle (a past-tense form of a verb; for example, *convicted* or *stolen*). This is the only element that always appears in passive voice.

3. The word *by*. This element is absent if the performer of the action is implied, unknown, or omitted.

Let's look at some passive sentences and their active counterparts. First, here's a passive sentence with all three of the elements listed above: a form of *to be* (*was*), a past participle (*chewed*), and *by*.

Passive
The writing book that covered passive voice <u>was chewed up by</u> the active police dog.

To make this sentence active, just switch things around. The writing book didn't chew up anything; the police dog did. So let's start with him.

Active
The active police dog chewed up the writing book that covered passive voice.

The next two examples contain just two elements of passive voice. The following passive construction includes a form of *to be* (*were*) and a past participle (*placed*).

Passive
Several banana peels <u>were placed</u> outside the suspect's house to slow him down.

Here the banana peels didn't do anything; some unnamed person used this clever tactic. When you make the sentence active, you clarify who put the peels there.

Active
The surveillance team placed several banana peels outside the suspect's house to slow him down.

This passive sentence contains a past participle (*left*) and the word *by*.

Passive
The judge tripped over the law books carelessly <u>left</u> lying around <u>by</u> the bailiff.

The law books aren't doing the action here; the bailiff is.

Active
The judge tripped over the law books the careless bailiff left lying around.

This last example contains only a past participle (*driven*).

Passive
<u>Driven</u> to the crime scene, the psychic led police to a viable suspect.

This sentence could confuse readers: They can't be sure if police drove the psychic to the crime scene, or if the power of a vision led her there. Let's make the sentence active and find out.

Active
After a dream drove the psychic to the crime scene, she helped police identify a viable suspect.

WHY YOU SHOULD AVOID PASSIVE VOICE

1. *Passive voice allows you to omit the subject (who is doing the action).* When you don't state who is doing what, readers don't know what you're talking about, especially if you leave out a *by* phrase to indicate who performed the action.

Passive
The rich <u>were stolen from</u> and the poor <u>given to</u>.

Who is stealing from the rich and giving to the poor? Let's specify who helped the less fortunate.

Active
Robin Hood stole from the rich and gave to the poor.

When you know who did what, you should use a clear subject. Sometimes, though, you don't know who did the action, or you're just talking in general. To avoid writing passively, try using *you* as the subject.

Passive
When a self-defense class <u>is taken</u>, it <u>can be learned</u> how to defend yourself against any attacker.

Active

When you take a self-defense class, you can learn how to defend yourself against any attacker.

Be sure not to use *you* too much. It's hard to say how many instances of *you* are too many—as the writer, you'll have to decide. Just make sure you vary your sentences.

2. *Passive voice forces you to use lots of weak* to be *verbs.* When most of your sentences are passive, you repeat dull verbs such as *was* and *were.* When you make your sentences active instead, you avoid using the same old verbs.

Passive

Someone who looked like the suspect <u>was rounded up</u>, but he <u>was released</u> after his alibi <u>was checked out</u>.

This sentence uses *was* three times. The active sentence, on the other hand, doesn't use *was* at all.

Active

The authorities rounded up someone who looked like the suspect, but they released him after checking out his alibi.

3. *Passive voice is wordy.* Passive voice forces you to use more words than necessary. When you make sentences active, you automatically save words.

Wordy

The officer who had starred in a movie about dancing detectives became incensed when it <u>was criticized by</u> the local paper.

Concise

The officer who had starred in a movie about dancing detectives became incensed when the local paper criticized it.

We'll talk a lot more about weak verbs in chapter four, and about wordiness in chapter seven.

WHEN IT'S OKAY TO USE PASSIVE VOICE

It's better to use active sentences, but use passive voice if:

1. You want to focus on the object, not the subject.

> The serial killer, who had stumped police for years, <u>was finally caught</u>.

This sentence focuses on the murderer, not on the police who caught him.

2. You don't care who did what, it's obvious who did it, or you don't know who did it.

> The department's new policy states that only candidates with police training <u>will be hired</u>; experience watching cop shows doesn't count.

It's obvious the department will be hiring the candidates.

3. You intend to omit who did what.

> Mistakes <u>were made</u> in the investigation.

The police or the detectives don't want to admit they investigated badly. This is a more roundabout way of saying *We made mistakes.*

You don't want to automatically eliminate all passive voice, just most of it.

RECAP

1. Underline all past participles (words such as *done* and *broken*). Also underline any forms of the verb *to be* (*am, is, are, was, were, be, being, been*) and the word *by* if you see them in a sentence with a past participle.

2. Identify who is doing the action (subject) and who is receiving it (object). Decide if you want to focus on the subject or the object. If the subject is most important, change the unwanted passive voice to active voice. Ensure the person or thing doing the action is the subject of the sentence. It's okay to leave a few passives here and there, if they serve a rhetorical purpose.

PASSIVE SENTENCES	BETTER SENTENCES
Awards for outstanding police work <u>were received by</u> Amy Arrestalot and Brian Behindbars.	Amy Arrestalot and Brian Behindbars received awards for outstanding police work.
The <u>forged</u> diploma was full of <u>misspelled</u> words, so the high-paying job <u>was not attained</u>.	The dropout misspelled a bunch of words in the diploma he forged, so he didn't get the high-paying job.

The mini-mart <u>was knocked over</u>, apparently for its delicious coffee.	The mini-mart was knocked over, apparently for its delicious coffee.*

* It's okay to use passive voice in this case because you don't know who stole the coffee. You could write *Someone knocked over the mini-mart*, but the original is better.

Exercise

It's your turn to detect and correct some passive voice. Reread the mystery at the beginning of this chapter, find all the passives, decide which ones are unnecessary, and then rewrite the story. Appendix two shows all the passives underlined and one way to rewrite the mystery. It's okay if your rewrite and the answer key don't match exactly.

SUMMARY

This chapter has introduced you to the concept of passive writing. You're now probably pretty good at detecting and correcting passive voice. The next time you compose something, try to remember to use active voice most of the time.

Chapter two discusses another type of passive writing called nominalization. Nominalizations are empty nouns that lead to the same problems you encountered here: vague subjects, weak verbs, and wordy sentences.

Chapter Two

THE ILLUMINATING INVESTIGATION INTO THE NASTY NOMINALIZATION

Detective Pinkersolve was ready for the selection of her next case. The decision to study Miss Crustlepuff's file was made because this might be her only opportunity to see the spinster's opulent villa.

An examination of the facts revealed a mystery whose solution could be reached only through superb detecting. Astonishment by Miss Crustlepuff had occurred upon the realization that a thief had absconded with her TV and toaster. However, the perpetrator's leaving of the heirloom silverware caused much head scratching. After a look-around of the grounds, the spinster puzzled over the two huge footprints near the service entrance.

Following a conversation with Miss Crustlepuff, Detective Pinkersolve felt confidence the case was nearing completion. The spinster knew only one person with enormous feet: a recently let-go employee. The questioning of the ex-maid revealed that she had wanted to pawn the silver, but its heaviness prevented removal. The carrying off of the small TV and extremely light toaster happened instead. She claimed the theft was necessary because she needed money for the purchase of some extra-large shoes. Although the items were returned, the ex-maid learned true repentance only after spending time in jail.

ominalizations are another passive writing style. They can lead to unclear, monotonous, or wordy sentences. You might not have heard the fancy term *nominalizations*, but you probably use these nouns when you write. Think of them as empty nouns that give no information about who did what. When you rewrite nominalizations, your sentences become clear and specific instead of vague.

HOW TO DETECT AND CORRECT NOMINALIZATIONS

Chances are, nominalizations are a new concept for you. Don't worry. You'll get the hang of them by the time you're done with this chapter. A nominalization is a noun you've created from a verb or adjective.

Nominalization
The screeching unnerved the rookie.

Screeching is a noun form of the verb *to screech*. This sentence is weak because readers don't know who is screeching. When you use the verb *to screech*, you give yourself room to identify the noisemaker.

Better
The uncooperative suspect screeched, unnerving the rookie.

Just like passive voice, nominalizations contain up to three elements. Sometimes you see only one or two of them; other times, all three appear.

---

1. A word such as *a*, *an*, *the*, *his*, *her*, *these*, or *several*.

2. A noun such as *utilization*, *sadness*, or *taking*. This is the only element that always appears in nominalizations.

3. The word *of*.

Let's look at some nominalizations and then some improved sentences. This nominalization contains all three of the elements listed above.

Nominalization
The last step was <u>the collection of</u> the victim's dust bunnies.

Here the verb *to collect* has become the noun *collection*. This sentence is vague because it doesn't specify who is collecting the evidence. All becomes clear when you use the verb *to collect* as well as a specific subject.

Better
The forensics team collected the victim's dust bunnies just before leaving the scene.

Now let's do an examination of—oops, I mean let's examine—a nominalization with two elements.

Nominalization
The senior citizen responded to the would-be robber with <u>an exclamation</u>: "Get your hands off my dentures!"

Here the verb *to exclaim* has become the noun *exclamation*. Let's improve the sentence.

Better

The senior citizen exclaimed to the would-be robber, "Get your hands off my dentures!"

Finally, here's a nominalization with just one element.

Nominalization

<u>Happiness</u> was evident after the clown was arrested.

The sentence is poor because it fails to mention who is happy.

Better

The detective was happy after she arrested the clown.

Nouns that end in *-tion* and *-ing* are often nominalizations. Even the word *nominalization* is a nominalization (it comes from the verb *to nominalize*).

WHY YOU SHOULD AVOID NOMINALIZATIONS

1. *Nominalizations allow you to omit the subject.* When you don't say who is doing the action, your sentences become vague. If instead you specify who is doing what, readers know exactly what you're talking about.

Nominalization

<u>The presentation of</u> the award was a proud moment.

The subject here is the empty noun *presentation*. This sentence leaves readers wondering what's going on. Who is presenting the award? Who is receiving it? What award are we talking about? Who is proud? You can clear up all these mysteries if you use *to present* as the sentence's verb and add the missing subject.

Better
The squad's best report writer proudly presented his partner with the Fewest Nominalizations award.

Sometimes you don't know who is doing what. Other times you're just discussing something in general and no specific person is doing the action. To avoid a nominalization, make *you* the subject.

Nominalization
One way to combat shoplifting is <u>the positioning of</u> security cameras in all corners of a store.

Better
You can combat shoplifting by positioning security cameras in all corners of a store.

Even better
Shop owners can combat shoplifting by positioning security cameras in all corners of their stores.

Be sure not to use *you* too much. Although there are no rules about how many instances of *you* are too many, your goal should be to vary your sentence structure so you don't bore the reader.

When you get rid of *things* as your subjects, you can put some life into the *people* you're writing about.

2. *Nominalizations often force you to use weak verbs.* Vague subjects go hand in hand with basic but weak verbs such as *to be* and *to do*. Although these verbs are integral parts of English, your writing can get rather monotonous if every sentence contains a *was* or *were*. When you rewrite nominalizations, you can almost always use better verbs—verbs that are colorful, add life and texture, and intrigue readers. Compare the verbs (in italics) in the sentences below.

Nominalization
The snapping of mug shots *was* really enjoyable for the officer.

Better
The officer really *enjoyed* snapping mug shots.

Even better
The officer *had a ball* snapping mug shots.

In the first example, the weak verb is *was. Enjoyed* is a much stronger verb, and the idiom *had a ball* is even more colorful and engaging.

Nominalizations and passive voice sometimes appear in the same sentence. You can fix both problems simultaneously.

3. *Nominalizations are often wordy.* When you reword nominalizations, your sentences usually become more concise.

Wordy

The recommendation of Internal Affairs was that the department suspend the cop because she ran out of gas during the high-speed chase. (23 words)

Concise

Internal Affairs recommended the department suspend the cop because she ran out of gas during the high-speed chase. (19 words)

We'll talk a lot more about weak verbs in chapter four, and about wordiness in chapter seven.

WHEN IT'S OKAY TO USE NOMINALIZATIONS

You should use a specific subject in most cases. However, a nominalization is acceptable if you don't know who is doing the action, or if the subject is unimportant.

The disappearance of every rat in town puzzled the police.

Perhaps the police should check the alibi of the Pied Piper....

RECAP

1. Underline all phrases in the form of *a preparation of* or *the sadness of*. Also sniff around for any nominalizations that don't use *of*. Underline them too.

2. If the sentence begins with a nominalization, check to see if you've used a weak verb, such as a form of *to be* or *to do*.

3. Rewrite the sentence. Figure out what verb or adjective to use instead of the nominalization. For example, *a preparation of* becomes the verb *to prepare*, and *the sadness of* becomes the adjective *sad*. Use this verb or adjective when you rewrite. You may need a new subject, so be sure to specify who or what is doing the action.

4. Smooth out the sentence if necessary.

VAGUE OR UNCLEAR SENTENCES	BETTER SENTENCES
<u>Several sightings of</u> the burly cops in pink sunglasses were noted by concerned citizens.	Several citizens became concerned when they spotted the burly cops in pink sunglasses.
The hungry Chief couldn't believe <u>the ineptitude of</u> the police officers who bought cupcakes instead of donuts.	The hungry Chief couldn't believe that the inept police officers bought cupcakes instead of donuts.
<u>The sentencing</u> was a disaster.	When the judge sentenced the grandma to hard time, the courtroom crowd rioted.

Exercise

It's your turn to detect and correct some nominalizations. Reread the mystery at the beginning of this chapter, find all the nominalizations, and then rewrite the story. Appendix two shows all the nominalizations underlined and one way to rewrite the mystery. It's okay if your rewrite and the answer key don't match exactly.

SUMMARY

You've seen how nominalizations can lead to vague sentences with repetitive verbs such as *was* and *were*. Next time you write, take a few extra seconds to clarify in your mind who is doing what. Then choose specific subjects and verbs. Before you know it, you won't be using nominalizations anymore.

Chapter three discusses another type of passive writing that leads to unclear or dull sentences: vague *-ing* words.

Chapter Three

THE PECULIAR PUZZLE OF THE VAGUE *-ING* WORD

The main clue that you've used a vague *-ing* word:

- Your sentence contains a word ending in *-ing* but you haven't stated who is doing the action.

Something stood out immediately while leafing through the stack of cases. "Oh, poor Monsieur Gourmand," sympathized Detective Pinkersolve.

Solving this assault with a dessert fork was a priority because snacking on éclairs from Monsieur Gourmand's patisserie, Le Chocolate Moose, was enjoyable when not working. Questioning the witness led to information that the crime occurred while preparing some chocolate-filled delights. Two vital clues were then uncovered when pointing out an abandoned razor near the scene and hinting that the new waiter might be involved.

Next up was interviewing Mr. Goostache, the unkempt waiter. Arguing with Monsieur Gourmand over his appearance had caused Mr. Goostache to defend his crumb-filled facial hair when seeing a razor in his hand. Stabbing his boss wasn't intended, but shaving wasn't an option. Perhaps combing his moustache better when next getting ready for work would be a good idea.

Closing the case was accomplished after giving the detective a free éclair and deciding not to file charges. Finding another waiter who could speak with a fake French accent wouldn't be easy. Her work here was done after thanking Monsieur Gourmand for the opportunity to serve—and to eat.

I f you successfully completed the first two lessons, you're now starting to use specific subjects and better verbs instead of passive sentence structure. This chapter continues investigating how to turn hard-to-follow writing into clear, easy-to-understand sentences. The culprit in this chapter is what we'll call vague -*ing* words. Follow the clues to learn how to correct this kind of passive writing.

HOW TO DETECT AND CORRECT VAGUE -*ING* WORDS

Words that end in -*ing* are very common in English. Many, such as the ones in the examples below, are perfectly fine.

- The hoodlum was <u>hoping</u> police wouldn't notice his mismatched socks.

- The <u>arresting</u> officer was less <u>dashing</u> than the juvenile delinquent.

- I like <u>visiting</u> the morgue on dreary days.

You don't need to worry about -*ing* words like these. However, you do need to look for vague and unspecific -*ing* words. Like sentences constructed with passive voice and nominalizations, sentences with vague -*ing* words are often missing clear subjects. Let's look at the following sentence.

Vague
<u>Burning down</u> the Stinky Foot Emporium was harder than anticipated.

This sentence doesn't tell readers who tried to burn down the shoe store. It's better to state the subject explicitly so readers know who did what.

Specific
The inexperienced arsonist had trouble burning down the Stinky Foot Emporium.

Sometimes unwanted -*ing* words pop up in the middle of a sentence.

Vague
The getaway van pulled away too fast, so <u>jumping</u> into the vehicle led to bruises.

In this sentence, the -*ing* word happens to be hiding in the middle, but you could have also written, *Jumping into the vehicle led to bruises because the getaway van pulled away too fast*. In either case, readers can't tell who got bruised. Specify a clear subject.

Specific
The getaway van pulled away too fast, so the bungling burglar got bruised when he jumped into it.

When you write a sentence that begins with an -*ing* word, a flag should go up. You may be forgetting to state who is doing the action. Vague -*ing* words in the middle of a sentence are less obvious. Wherever you see an -*ing* word, ask yourself, *Have I included a subject here?*

Vague *-ing* words often surface after one of these words or phrases: *after, although, before, by, due to, if, instead of, since, though, through, upon, when, whereas,* and *while.*

Vague
The officer realized some vital evidence had gotten lost <u>while eating</u> lunch.

This sentence makes it sound like the evidence was nibbling a sandwich. Let's rewrite it and clarify who was eating.

Specific
While the officer was eating lunch, he realized he'd lost some vital evidence.

In chapter five, which covers misplaced modifiers, we'll talk a lot more about problematic sentences that contain vague *-ing* words. Don't worry about misplaced modifiers right now. Just look out for *-ing* words that appear with one of the clue words or phrases. Then make sure a clear subject accompanies each one.

WHY YOU SHOULD AVOID VAGUE *-ING* WORDS

1. *Vague -ing words allow you to omit the subject (who is doing what).* Readers have trouble deciphering vague sentences. Spend a few extra seconds establishing a specific subject.

Missing subject
<u>Leaving</u> a trail of white pebbles was how they outwitted their evil stepmother, who wanted them dead.

Readers have no idea who is leaving a trail of white pebbles; nor do they know who *they* refers to. Readers could guess, but it's better to specify what you mean. In this case, you don't even need to delete the *-ing* word to clarify the subject.

Clear subject
By leaving a trail of white pebbles, Hansel and Gretel outwitted their evil stepmother, who wanted them dead.

Here's another example.

Missing subject
Much has happened <u>since breaking out of</u> prison to buy that fantastic writing book.

Who broke out of prison? Let's find out.

Clear subject
Much has happened to the inmate since he broke out of prison to buy that fantastic writing book.

When you're replacing a vague *-ing* construction with a clear subject and verb, you can often use another form of the verb that appears in the vague *-ing* construction. For example, turn *since breaking out of prison* into *since he broke out of prison*.

Some vague *-ing* words can be doubly confusing if there are two possible subjects.

Ambiguous
The arsonist caught the thief <u>while hiding</u> the murder weapon.

Was the arsonist or the thief hiding the murder weapon? In this case, you can solve the problem by being more specific about who is performing the action indicated by the *-ing* word.

Clear
The arsonist caught the thief, who was hiding the murder weapon.

Clear
While the arsonist was hiding the murder weapon, he caught the thief.

If you don't know who is doing what, or you're talking in general terms, you can use *you* as the subject to avoid writing a vague sentence. If that won't work—or if the *you* sentence structure is becoming too repetitive—rewrite the sentence and come up with a clear subject.

2. *Vague* -ing *words at the beginning of a sentence force you to use weak verbs.* Basic verbs like *to be* and *to do* can get rather monotonous. When you specify who is doing what, you can use more interesting verbs, too. Compare the verbs (in italics) in the sentences below.

Weak verb
Working in a graveyard *isn't* such a bad job.

Better verb
I *dig* working in a graveyard.

The verb *dig* in the second sentence is much clearer and more colorful than the verb *isn't* in the first. We'll talk a lot more about weak verbs in chapter four.

If you need to write something that's not very exciting to read, such as a computer manual or a memo about human resources policies, don't bore readers any more than necessary. Try to use specific rather than vague language.

WHEN IT'S OKAY TO USE VAGUE *-ING* WORDS

It's always best to state who is doing what. However, you can use vague *-ing* words if:

1. *It's clear who or what is performing the action.*

> The lab's delivery boy dropped the fiber evidence into his soda
> while trying to simultaneously drive and snack. Fishing it out
> before it was ruined was impossible.

The context makes it clear who was trying to drive, eat, and rescue the evidence.

2. *You want to be vague on purpose.*

> Going about his everyday business was part of his cover. It
> seemed he was a nice enough fellow, but he was really the
> one who'd eaten all of Wanda's goldfish.

Mystery writers can get away with using vague sentence structure to hide a perpetrator's identity. Most writers, however, should avoid vague sentences.

RECAP

1. Underline *-ing* words that begin a sentence. Look out for vague *-ing* words elsewhere in the sentence as well.

2. Underline *-ing* words that follow one of these words or phrases: *after*, *although*, *before*, *by*, *due to*, *if*, *instead of*, *since*, *though*, *through*, *upon*, *when*, *whereas*, and *while*.

3. Determine which sentences with *-ing* words are missing a clear subject. Rewrite each sentence and state who or what is performing the action of the *-ing* word. You can often use another form of the verb that appears in the vague *-ing* construction (for example, turn *after going* into *after he goes*). Try to use a more interesting verb than *was* or *were*.

VAGUE SENTENCES	BETTER SENTENCES
<u>Cowering</u> in the neighbor's bushes after a robbery is ill advised, especially with bad knees.	Criminals shouldn't cower in the bushes after robbing a neighbor, especially if they have bad knees.
The ink needs to be applied to fingers <u>when getting</u> a suspect's prints; <u>taking</u> toe prints isn't allowed.	When you are getting a suspect's prints, apply the ink to his fingers; you're not allowed to take toe prints.

Finding signs that trained elephants had invaded the peanut factory led to an arrest.	After the astute security guard found signs that trained elephants had invaded the peanut factory, he arrested the animal trainer.

Exercise

It's your turn to detect and correct some vague *-ing* words. Reread the mystery at the beginning of this chapter, find all the vague *-ing* words, then rewrite the story. Appendix two shows all the vague *-ing* words underlined and one way to rewrite the mystery. It's okay if your rewrite and the answer key don't match exactly.

SUMMARY

You now know how to avoid three common kinds of passive writing: passive voice, nominalizations, and vague *-ing* words. You have also learned the importance of crafting sentences with clear subjects and verbs. In the next chapter, we'll discuss another way to eliminate imprecise language: how to select better and more specific verbs.

Chapter Four

THE DELICIOUS DRAMA
OF THE WEAK VERB

> Clues that you've used a weak verb:
>
> - forms of *to be*: *am, is, are, was, were, be, being, been*
> - forms of other weak verbs: *to do, to get, to go, to have, to make, to occur, to use*

Detective Pinkersolve's next case involved a man who may have been poisoned. His gastric symptoms got better, but he didn't know what had made him ill. There were no unusual chemicals lying about the house. He hoped it wasn't arsenic poisoning.

He thought it was possible his new dog walker was guilty because they had recently argued. Apparently Miss Poodlepull didn't want to walk Pookie around the block ten times. It was tiring, so she went around only eight times. When Detective Pinkersolve talked with Miss Poodlepull, it was clear she was too busy to poison anyone. There were nine dogs for her to walk each day.

It was time to close the case. There were some questions asked and some revealing answers given. The detective learned that the man's grandson, a student at the culinary institute, had recently cooked some meals for him. It was certain that a new recipe from Sonny's oyster class had caused the stomach pains. Sonny was very sorry. He offered to make the two of them a special meal to make up for all the trouble. Both quickly said that there were other things they had to do. It was time for Detective Pinkersolve to move on to her next case.

W e've spent three chapters learning how to write clear subjects. Now we'll focus solely on verbs. Forms of the verb *to be* and other basic verbs weaken sentences. Choose colorful, clear, strong, precise, and active verbs instead of vague, monotonous, and run-of-the-mill verbs. You don't need to search the thesaurus, use difficult vocabulary, or change every weak verb, however. Just select specific, descriptive verbs that communicate exactly what you mean to say. Vibrant verbs are more exciting to read—and to write—than plain ones.

HOW TO DETECT AND CORRECT WEAK VERBS

Weak verbs are everyday, normal verbs we use all the time. However, they're often repetitive, passive, wordy, or too general. These verbs frequently fail to clarify the action, and they make readers work too hard.

Let's start with the most common offender, the verb *to be* (its forms are: *am, is, are, was, were, be, being,* and *been*). Even when you've cut down on passive voice, nominalizations, and vague *-ing* words, verbs such as *was* and *were* can still inundate your writing.

Weak
The misplaced-tiger case <u>was</u> time-consuming to solve.

This sentence isn't incorrect, but it is boring and not very specific. See how much better the sentence becomes when you get rid of the *was*.

Stronger
The cops stayed up all night hunting down the misplaced tiger.

To be verbs crop up in phrases such as *there were*, *it is*, and *this was*. The chart below lists common *to be* constructions.

THERE	IT	THIS
there is	it is	this is
there's	it's	this was
there are	it was	this has been
there was	it has been	this will be
there were	it will be	
there has been		
there have been		
there will be		

You can almost always rewrite these bland phrases.

Weak
<u>There's</u> a good reason why the con failed: The criminal forgot that Mrs. Uppercrust <u>was</u> the target.

Stronger
Why did the con fail? The criminal forgot to target Mrs. Uppercrust.

Other basic but boring verbs—such as *to do*, *to get*, *to go*, *to have*, *to make*, *to occur*, and *to use*—are often too general. They also lack spice.

Weak
He <u>did</u> the crime so he could <u>get</u> enough money for a new watch.

Pick verbs that are more specific and descriptive.

Stronger
He stole from Grandpa so he could splurge on a new watch.

WHY YOU SHOULD AVOID WEAK VERBS

1. *Weak verbs can be unclear, especially if you use* there is *and* it is. Weak verbs tend to be general and ho-hum. Specific verbs allow you to describe exactly what nuance you want to relay.

Weak
<u>There were</u> bees everywhere, so the officer <u>was</u> nervous during the stakeout.

This sentence is dull and unspecific. Let's improve it.

Stronger
Bees buzzed all around the officer during the stakeout, so he nervously flapped his arms.

To buzz around and *to flap* are vibrant verbs that clarify the officer's actions. When you rewrite weak *to be* or other verbs, you don't have to use a thesaurus to come up with difficult words. You want to avoid using distracting vocabulary that readers will notice. Instead of using pompous words, aim for precise verbs that relay your message well.

2. *Weak verbs bore readers.* When you rely on the same verbs over and over, your writing becomes monotonous. *To be* is such a basic verb that you could probably use a form of it in every sentence. However, readers have seen *is, are, was,* and *were* thousands of times. Specific verbs add variety.

Weak
It <u>was</u> impossible for the robber on roller skates to stop as he <u>went</u> downhill.

Stronger
When the robber on roller skates fled downhill, he discovered he couldn't stop.

You sometimes have to change your sentence around to accommodate a better verb. This can be a little hard at first, but it'll get easier with some practice.

3. *Weak verbs often lead to wordy sentences.* When you use weak sentence structure along with a form of the verb *to be*, your sentences can become a bit bloated.

Wordy
<u>There is</u> one particular bank <u>that</u> criminals like to hit because the walls <u>are</u> money green. (16 words)

Concise
Criminals always hit this particular bank because of its money-green walls. (12 words)

Many wordy sentences contain the word *that* along with a form of *to be*. The word *that* is often extraneous, so you can usually chop it out when rewriting a weak verb.

WHEN IT'S OKAY TO USE WEAK VERBS

You've probably noticed that this book contains its share of *to be* and other so-so verbs. The point of this chapter is not that you should eliminate every weak verb. However, you can spruce up all kinds of writing—not just fiction—here and there by replacing weak verbs with stronger, more colorful, and more specific verbs. When you're reviewing what you've written, select a few spots where a better verb would clarify what you're saying.

Don't get all fancy and use pompous language; just try to avoid using too many basic verbs.

RECAP

1. Underline all forms of *to be*. Look out for weak phrasing such as *there is, it is*, and *this is*.

2. Underline other weak-sounding verbs such as *to do, to get, to go, to have, to make*, and *to use*.

3. Rewrite some of the underlined verbs. Choose spots where you can use more specific or more descriptive words. You may need to rearrange your sentence to accommodate your improved verbs.

POOR SENTENCES	BETTER SENTENCES
This police hangout <u>is</u> the rookies' favorite because the bartender <u>is</u> generous after 11 P.M.	This police hangout rocks because the bartender gives free drinks to rookies after 11 P.M.

<u>There was</u> a great comedy about mountaineering Mounties, so we <u>went</u> to see it.	We laughed our heads off at the movie about mountaineering Mounties.
When the officer tried to <u>use</u> her ATM card, a problem <u>occurred</u>.	When the officer tried to withdraw money from the ATM, she discovered she'd blown it all.

Exercise

It's your turn to detect and correct some weak verbs. Reread the mystery at the beginning of this chapter, find all the weak verbs, and then rewrite the story with more descriptive ones. Appendix two shows all the weak verbs underlined and one way to rewrite the mystery. It's okay if your rewrite and the answer key don't match exactly.

SUMMARY

This chapter has shown you how to identify and replace weak verbs. When you use less common verbs instead of the same old ones, you'll communicate your ideas more clearly and uniquely.

So far we've covered subjects and verbs. Next we'll investigate misplaced modifiers—descriptive phrases that end up next to the wrong word.

Chapter Five

THE CURIOUS CASE OF
THE MISPLACED MODIFIER

A modifier is a word or short phrase that describes something. In the following sentence, the underlined phrase is a modifier that describes *the cop*.

Sad to be leaving the force, the cop cried at his retirement party.

Modifying words and phrases usually describe the nearest noun. A misplaced modifier is a modifier that ends up next to the wrong word. In the sentence below, the underlined modifier seems to be describing *a retirement party*.

Sad to be leaving the force, a retirement party was held for the cop, who cried.

Gazing outside, it occurred to Detective Pinkersolve that she was nearly done with her cases. Off to interview a witness from a recent carjacking caper, there was no time to lose.

The witness had seen a man trying to carjack a woman brandishing a weapon. Looking around for another vehicle because he couldn't drive a stick shift, a pizza delivery bike soon came by that sported a Slow Poke Pizza sign. While munching on a cold slice, police put out an APB for a man with an anchovy on his face who was cycling slowly.

Upset that the culprit got away, a wanted poster was drawn that Detective Pinkersolve hoped would help capture him. The detective needed to think about the case, so she ordered some pizza from Slow Poke's that would undoubtedly be delicious. After waiting two hours, the pizza finally came. Something struck her that was odd. Jack, the delivery cyclist, looked just like the composite sketch of the bike-jacker! Admitting he was the suspect, jail was avoided. Explaining how, Slow Poke's generous manager was allowing Jack to work off his debt to society. Detective Pinkersolve decided to withhold a tip and began working her next case.

Descriptive words and phrases, also known as modifiers, bring your writing to life—but only if you put them in the right place, which is almost always right next to what they describe. When modifiers end up next to the wrong word, they're called misplaced modifiers. Misplaced modifiers lead to nonsensical, confusing, or even unintentionally funny sentences.

To modify means "to describe." At their most basic, modifiers are single-word adjectives. *Happy* and *inquisitive* are adjectives and therefore modifiers. However, modifiers can come in lots of other configurations, including whole phrases. They can be tough to identify at first, especially if you're not used to looking for them. This chapter covers the most common types of modifiers you'll encounter, and shows you many examples. Before long, you'll have no problem putting your modifiers where they belong.

This chapter uses a few more grammar terms than previous chapters. If you're ever unsure what a term means, use the glossary to refresh your memory.

HOW TO DETECT AND CORRECT MISPLACED MODIFIERS (BEGINNING OF A SENTENCE)

When a modifier starts a sentence, it needs to match up with what comes immediately *after* it. A modifier that begins a sentence often takes the form of a short group of words that ends in a comma. Follow these clues to identify the most common kinds of modifiers—and misplaced modifiers—at the beginning of a sentence.

1. *The sentence begins with an* -ing *word.* Words ending in *-ing* at the beginning of a sentence often turn out to be misplaced modifiers.

> **Misplaced modifier**
> <u>Realizing she was lost</u>, it occurred to the policewoman that she should pull the motorist over to ask for directions.

Here the modifier, *Realizing she was lost*, mistakenly describes *it*, which comes directly after the comma. This sentence could confuse readers because *it* didn't do any realizing. Put *the policewoman* right after the modifier.

> **Better**
> Realizing she was lost, the policewoman pulled the motorist over to ask for directions.

2. *The second or third word of the sentence is an* -ing *word.* The following words or phrases often precede an *-ing* word: *after, although, before, by, due to, if, instead of, since, though, through, upon, when, whereas,* and *while.* If your sentence begins with one of these words or phrases followed by an *-ing* word, check to make sure that the modifier describes what comes after it.

> **Misplaced modifier**
> <u>After robbing the bank</u>, a plane took the thief to the Bahamas.

The modifier, *After robbing the bank*, mistakenly describes *a plane*, which directly follows the comma. It sure would be hard for a plane to rob a bank!

Better
After robbing the bank, the thief flew to the Bahamas.

3. *The sentence begins with a past participle.* A past participle is a past-tense form of a verb: *typed*, *broken*. (Feel free to review the discussion of past participles in chapter one, if you'd like.)

Misplaced modifier
<u>Hurried out of the courtroom by the bailiff</u>, the yodel was off-key.

The modifier that contains a past participle, *Hurried out of the courtroom by the bailiff*, mistakenly describes *the yodel*. This sentence will surely make readers smile. You can fix the problem by clarifying who did what.

Better
Hurried out of the courtroom by the bailiff, the yodeling defendant sang off-key.

You could improve this sentence further by getting rid of the passive voice (*hurried ... by the bailiff*).

Even better
The yodeling defendant sang off-key while the bailiff hurried him out of the courtroom.

4. *The sentence starts with* as, like, *or* unlike.

Misplaced modifier

<u>As a law-abiding citizen</u>, red lights never get run when I'm around.

The modifier *As a law-abiding citizen* mistakenly describes *red lights*. (Perhaps the cops are extra strict in that town, so both people and traffic signals obey the law.) Put the modifier next to what it describes.

Better

As a law-abiding citizen, I never run red lights.

The words *it* and *there* often appear after the comma when misplaced modifiers begin a sentence.

HOW TO DETECT AND CORRECT MISPLACED MODIFIERS (MIDDLE OR END OF A SENTENCE)

Now let's look at modifiers that appear in the middle or at the end of a sentence. These modifiers can be difficult to spot because they're mixed in with the other parts of the sentence. When a modifier falls in the middle or at the end of a sentence, it needs to match up with what comes directly *before* it. Follow these clues to detect common modifiers—and misplaced modifiers—in the middle or at the end of a sentence.

1. *A phrase or clause starts with* that. *That* phrases and clauses, when used as modifiers, describe things or animals (but not people).

Misplaced modifier

The uniform she wore yesterday <u>that is splattered with mustard</u> needs to be washed.

Notice that *yesterday* comes right before the modifier, *that is splattered with mustard*. *Yesterday* is not stained with mustard. Also note how the *that* clause interrupts the sentence's flow. Unfortunately, there's no easy way to move the word *uniform* next to the word *that*. The best way to improve this sentence is to rephrase it.

Better

The uniform she wore yesterday is splattered with mustard, so she needs to wash it.

2. *A phrase or clause starts with* who. *Who* phrases and clauses describe people (but not things or animals).

Misplaced modifier

The beggar at the park <u>who tried to pick my pocket</u> needed a spray of perfume.

The modifier, *who tried to pick my pocket*, mistakenly describes *the park*. *Who* clauses should describe people, so it's confusing when *the park* comes before *who*.

Better

The beggar who tried to pick my pocket when I was at the park needed a spray of perfume.

3. *A phrase or clause could start with* that *or* who, *but this word has been left out.* Many times you can omit *that* or *who* because the reader will infer it from the context.

The modifier here is *I honked at*, but you could have
written *who I honked at* (or, if you are very formal, *at
whom I honked*). With or without *who*, the modifier
mistakenly describes *the ugly coat*. It's rather silly to
honk at a coat.

WHY YOU ACCIDENTALLY MISPLACE YOUR MODIFIERS

Misplaced modifiers are extremely common and appear in almost all writing, no matter what the topic.
One way to avoid this problem is to watch out for its
common causes. You're more likely to misplace your
modifiers when:

1. *You're thinking on the fly and writing whatever comes
to mind.* You may sometimes write without completely
thinking things through. Other times you may need to
jot your thoughts down quickly so you don't forget your
ideas. When you're in a hurry, you're less likely to check
your sentence structure.

This sentence is half-baked. The writer was probably thinking about eating cookies instead of concentrating on the sentence structure. To fix this nonsensical sentence, move *lovingly baked by her husband* next to what it's supposed to modify: *some delicious cookies.*

Better
The officer brought some delicious cookies, lovingly baked by her husband, to the party.

Be suspicious of sentences that begin with a short group of words followed by a comma. A misplaced modifier might be lurking.

2. *You're trying to fit too much into your sentence.* If you try to stack two modifiers together to describe a noun, the second modifier may end up describing something in the first modifier instead of what it's supposed to describe.

Misplaced modifier
As Mike was about to get fingerprinted, he noticed that the officer with the ink pad was a buddy he hadn't seen in ages who had helped him escape from juvenile hall years ago.

Here the two modifiers are *he hadn't seen in ages* (a modifier that could begin with *who*) and *who had helped him escape from juvenile hall years ago.* Both of these apply to *a buddy.* You can fix the sentence by breaking it in two.

Two sentences

As Mike was about to get fingerprinted, he noticed that the officer with the ink pad was a buddy he hadn't seen in ages. Mike fondly remembered how Bill had helped him escape from juvenile hall years ago.

You could also move or rewrite one of the modifiers.

Rewritten modifier

As Mike was about to get fingerprinted, he noticed that the officer with the ink pad was the long-lost buddy who had helped him escape from juvenile hall years ago.

Another mistake you may make when trying to fit too much into a sentence is separating the noun from its modifier with extra words or a phrase. Often, the interloper is what's called a prepositional phrase—a phrase that begins with a preposition such as *in* or *by*. In the sentence below, the prepositional phrase *down the alley* falls between the noun and the modifier.

Misplaced modifier

The cop chased a young man down the alley <u>who was trying to carry off two heavy bags of nickels</u>.

Down the alley separates the noun *man* from its modifier, the clause beginning with *who*. The man, not the alley, was trying to carry the money. One way to fix this sentence is to reword the sentence slightly and move the prepositional phrase.

Rewritten modifier

The cop ran down the alley as he chased a young man who was trying to carry off two heavy bags of nickels.

You could also break the sentence in two.

Two sentences
The cop chased a robber down the alley. The delinquent was trying to carry off two heavy bags of nickels.

At first it might seem hard to find a new home for an errant modifier. You're right; it is difficult. However, if a modifier is in the wrong place, you'll have to rewrite, even if it means you need to scrap what you've written and start over. So it's best not to get too attached to any particular sentence.

3. *The modifier is somewhat long, so you put it after the verb instead of before it.* Most of the time it's easy to spot misplaced modifiers such as these because they abruptly interrupt the sentence's flow.

Misplaced modifier
The police dog has been promoted <u>that chased the suspect all the way to the next town</u>.

You need to move the *that* clause next to *the police dog*.

Better
The police dog that chased the suspect all the way to the next town has been promoted.

RECAP

1. Find and underline all modifiers. They may fall at the beginning of the sentence, in the middle, or at the end. Modifiers at the beginning of a sentence are often followed by a comma.

2. If you find a modifier at the beginning of a sentence, circle what comes immediately after the modifier. If you find a modifier in the middle or at the end of a sentence, circle what comes directly before the modifier.

3. Underline what the modifier is supposed to describe. (If the noun that the modifier is supposed to describe is missing, write it in the margin.)

4. If the words you circled in step two and underlined in step three are not the same word, then you have a misplaced modifier. Rewrite the sentence so that the modifier and the true subject are right next to each other. You may need to rearrange or reword the sentence.

POOR SENTENCES	BETTER SENTENCES
When detaining the suspect, the handcuffs somehow got attached to the officer's wrists.	When detaining the suspect, the officer somehow handcuffed the wrong person—himself.
Freshly painted, visitors can now admire the reopened police station.	Visitors can now admire the reopened police station, which has been freshly painted.
He wondered if any of the witnesses would come forward who saw the crime.	He wondered if any of the witnesses who saw the crime would come forward.

Exercise

It's your turn to detect and correct some misplaced modifiers. Reread the mystery at the beginning of this chapter, find all the misplaced modifiers, and then rewrite the story. Appendix two shows all the misplaced modifiers underlined and one way to rewrite the mystery. It's okay if your rewrite and the answer key don't match exactly.

SUMMARY

Modifiers can be a tricky bunch, but you now know how to keep them in their place. In the next chapter, you'll see how to cut overly long sentences down to size.

Chapter Six

THE CONFUSING CAPER CONCERNING THE SUPER-LONG SENTENCE

Detective Pinkersolve's next case involved identity theft, a fast-growing crime that was often hard to solve, and it bothered her—all crimes bothered her, actually, but this particular crime causes a huge hassle for its victims, who have to spend a long time straightening things out—because her neighbor (who was a florist) had been targeted.

When Miss Tuliptoes opened the mail, she discovered an astronomical credit card bill (she'd lost the card, along with some potting soil, just last week), and she needed the detective's help—living next to a detective sure was great! Credit 'R Us told the florist she wasn't responsible for the fraudulent charges—boy, was she relieved, since she was strapped for cash—and the detective promised to get on the case right away, but Miss Tuliptoes was actually glad someone had stolen her identity because she was tired of her name (she'd always wanted to change it, and this was the opportunity she'd been looking for). She didn't really want the detective to investigate, she admitted—she just wanted help picking a new name—and so they spent the morning testing out names until Detective Pinkersolve told whatever-her-name-was that she had to look into her next case.

I't's easy to write an extra-long sentence. You're making a very interesting point and you just keep going and going and going. Some writers fit four or five sentences into one with the help of certain words and lots of punctuation. Others succeed in making one sentence a whole paragraph. If you tend to create overly long sentences, this chapter will help you keep your sentences more manageable.

HOW TO DETECT AND CORRECT OVERLY LONG SENTENCES

Long sentences can befuddle readers. By the time they arrive at the end of the sentence, they've forgotten what came at the beginning. It's hard to define how many words are too many, because not all long sentences are too long. For our purposes, let's say that a forty-word sentence might be overly long. Twenty-five words are almost always enough. Here are three signs that a sentence is too long.

1. *The sentence consists of two longish sentences joined with* and *or* but. Sometimes you use a comma and the word *and* or *but* to link two sentences that could otherwise stand alone. It's fine to join two short sentences in this manner. However, if each of the two sentences is on the long side by itself, the resulting sentence might be hard to follow.

Unwieldy

The prisoner didn't mind that his cellmate liked to babble on about how he didn't get along with his in-laws during his entire six-month marriage, <u>but</u> Oscar decided to tune his buddy out when Rufus started going into detail about how his wife's mother never approved of his walrus mustache.

That's a lot of information in one sentence. Break it into two more readable sentences.

Manageable

The prisoner didn't mind that his cellmate liked to babble on about how he didn't get along with his in-laws during his entire six-month marriage. However, Oscar decided to tune his buddy out when Rufus started going into detail about how his wife's mother never approved of his walrus mustache.

One way to break up sentences joined with *and* is to end the sentence before the word *and*, delete the word *and*, and then start a new sentence with *In addition*. Or you can use *also* somewhere in the second sentence. For sentences linked with *but*, start the new sentence with *However*. If you want to be informal, use *And* or *But* at the beginning of the new sentence instead.

2. *The sentence contains lots of these words:* after, although, because, before, if, since, so, though, when, which, *and* who. These words are often preceded by a comma. Their presence may announce that you've gone off on a tangent—or four or five. If you include too many of these words, the resulting commas can get really confusing.

Unwieldy

<u>Although</u> the traffic-school instructor had wanted to be a comedian, <u>since</u> he was extremely funny <u>when</u> he joked about running red lights, <u>which</u> he probably did a lot <u>before</u> changing his driving habits and taking this teaching job, he told the class he wasn't very successful on the stand-up-comedy circuit.

This sentence is rather hard to follow. Go ahead and break it up.

Manageable

The traffic-school instructor had wanted to be a stand-up comedian. He was extremely funny when he joked about running red lights, which he probably did a lot before changing his driving habits and taking this teaching job. However, as he told the class, he wasn't very successful on the stand-up-comedy circuit.

To rewrite long sentences that contain many side thoughts, find the sentence's main idea and make that your primary sentence. Then create additional sentences out of the remaining thoughts.

3. *The sentence contains lots of punctuation marks.* In addition to commas, pairs of em dashes and parentheses pop up in overly long sentences. (An em dash is a long dash that announces a break in thought.) Writers sometimes use these punctuation marks to add a longish statement or an entire sentence to the middle of an existing sentence.

Unwieldy

The tracker that the department hired to sniff out a suspect in the desert—temperatures in this desert often reach 115 degrees in the shade, he warned us—demanded we foot the bill for the twenty gallons of water he wanted to lug along.

When readers see a whole sentence within em dashes or parentheses, they often have to skip what's within the punctuation marks, read ahead to the rest of the sentence, and then go back and read what they skipped. That's no fun. Create a version they won't need to reread.

Manageable

The tracker that the department hired to sniff out a suspect in the desert demanded we foot the bill for the twenty gallons of water he wanted to lug along. He warned us that temperatures in this desert often reach 115 degrees in the shade.

To fix sentences that contain too much material between em dashes or parentheses, cut what's between the punctuation marks. Then use what you cut to create a new sentence.

Keep in mind that a long sentence is not the same as a run-on sentence. A run-on sentence happens when you join two sentences with a comma instead of using a period, semicolon, or a conjunction (*and, but, or*).

Run-on sentence

The officer ate too many fries, he got a stomachache.

You can fix this by making the run-on sentence two sentences (just replace the comma with a period), or you can reword and make it one sentence.

Better
The officer ate too many fries, so he got a stomachache.

WHY YOU SHOULD AVOID OVERLY LONG SENTENCES

1. *Too much side information confuses readers.* Long sentences make readers work hard. If they lose the train of thought, they have to reread the sentence. As the writer, you'll have to judge how much side information is too much. Try to limit yourself to two or three thoughts per sentence. You can see in the examples below how the addition of each idea complicates the sentence and makes it more difficult to read.

One idea
The officer arrived late for the court hearing.

Two ideas
Although the officer had set his alarm, he arrived late for the court hearing.

Three ideas
Although the officer had set his alarm, which made a piercing siren sound, he arrived late for the court hearing.

This sentence is still fine, but it's getting a bit busy.

Four ideas
Although the officer had set his alarm, which made a piercing siren sound, he arrived late for the court hearing, at which he was testifying about his role in the bungled stakeout.

This last idea is just too much. It would be best to break this sentence up.

You sometimes have to be creative about how to reroute all the information you originally fit in one sentence. Try to put extra pieces of information elsewhere in your paragraph, or consider deleting something. No matter what you do with these extra bits, ensure you transition smoothly between thoughts. You don't want to end up with many short sentences that sound like a choppy list.

2. *Readers become confused when the subject is far from the verb.* When you add lots of side thoughts to a sentence's main idea, you may separate the subject and the verb by too many words. Readers may forget the subject before they get to the verb.

Confusing

Joanna, who was looking for a birthday present for her son (Andrew had just graduated from the police academy, and Joanna thought he could use a good instructional video), was browsing in her favorite store when an unusual title caught her eye: *Handcuff 'Em Like a Professional.*

Twenty-eight words separate the subject (*Joanna*) and the verb (*was browsing*). Break this sentence up to make it easier to follow.

Clear

Joanna needed to buy a birthday present for her son, who had just graduated from the police academy. She thought Andrew could use a good instructional video. As she browsed in her favorite store, an unusual title caught her eye: *Handcuff 'Em Like a Professional*.

Try to keep the subject and the verb near each other and separated by no more than one extra thought.

WHEN IT'S OKAY TO USE LONG SENTENCES

It's best to avoid huge sentences that contain too many thoughts. However, don't worry if long sentences surface once in a while. It's good to keep readers on their toes. To make your writing interesting, mix in some longish sentences with some short and medium-length ones.

RECAP

1. Start reading the sentence. If you forget what the beginning of the sentence is before you reach the end, it's probably too long. A very obvious way to tell you're being long-winded is if the period at the end is very far from the capital letter at the beginning. Also, take note when your word-processing program's grammar checker points out long sentences.

2. Underline all the words that can indicate you've put too much into the sentence: *and, but, after,*

although, because, before, if, since, so, though, when, which, and *who.* Underline pairs of em dashes and parentheses as well.

3. To shorten a sentence, start by figuring out the sentence's main idea. Use that as the basis for the primary sentence. Then find a place for the other parts of the overly long sentence. Chances are, you can turn these extra bits into two or three new sentences.

4. Make sure that the new sentences flow well together and that the transitions are smooth.

COMPLICATED SENTENCES	BETTER SENTENCES
When the woman hit the million-dollar jackpot (she had played the lottery faithfully for three years using the same numbers), she was so excited that she accidentally ran over the neighbor's cat, which had been lounging under her car, but she didn't notice the poor kitty until she got home from cashing the check.	The woman had played the lottery faithfully for three years using the same numbers. When she hit the million-dollar jackpot, she was so excited that she accidentally ran over the neighbor's cat, which had been lounging under her car. However, she didn't notice the poor kitty until she got home from cashing the check.

<u>Although</u> the officer needed to find four ladies <u>who</u> were willing to pose as bank robbers for a police lineup, <u>when</u> he asked his mom to volunteer—<u>which</u> she did gladly, <u>since</u> she always supported his efforts to reduce crime—he soon regretted his decision <u>because</u> the teller fingered her as the suspect.	The officer needed to find four ladies who were willing to pose as bank robbers for a police lineup. When he asked his mom to volunteer, she did so gladly, since she always supported his efforts to reduce crime. But he soon regretted his decision because the teller fingered his mom as the suspect.
The traffic cop (he'd been hiding under a tree <u>so</u> speeding motorists wouldn't see him, <u>which</u> ended up being a very effective tactic) was nearing the end of his shift—he'd nabbed eighteen speeders—<u>when</u> he realized he'd run out of blank tickets.	The traffic cop hid under a tree so speeding motorists wouldn't see him. His tactic was so effective that he nabbed eighteen speeders. But he ran out of blank tickets just before his shift ended.

Exercise

It's your turn to detect and correct some overly long sentences. Reread the mystery at the beginning of this chapter, find all the long sentences, and then rewrite the story. Appendix two shows

all the clue words underlined and then one way
to rewrite the mystery. It's okay if your rewrite
and the answer key don't match exactly.

SUMMARY

When you have a burst of inspiration, it's fine to write everything down all at once. However, when you review what
you've written, be sure to chop up long sentences to keep
them manageable. In the next chapter, you'll learn how to
enhance readability even more by reducing wordiness.

Chapter Seven

THE STRETCHED-OUT STORY OF THE WORDY WRITING

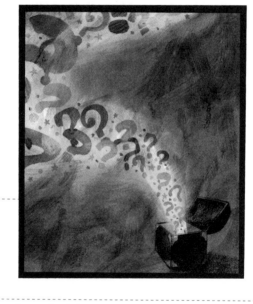

Clues that you're being too wordy:

- You've used a long-winded phrase.
- A form of *to be* or another weak verb appears in the sentence.
- You've repeated information.

Detective Pinkersolve's last case was one that dealt with graffiti. There had been numerous sightings by the townspeople of spray-paintings of scary dragons exhaling a phone number. The alarming thought that crossed the detective's mind was that there was a new gang that was recruiting new members with these dragons.

When the phone number was called, a mint company was reached. The receptionist's announcement was that this was the first call that had been received by the company. Detective Pinkersolve would therefore be the recipient of a free sample of the company's new Dragon Breath Mints. The explanation was that there was a new mint in town, not a new gang. It was explained that some local art students had been commissioned to advertise these new mints. However, the receptionist's explanation was that the company would have to do a reevaluation of this apparently unsuccessful campaign. The removal of all dragons would be done immediately. Detective Pinkersolve said she felt sure that the company had the capability of thinking of another advertising strategy. She then said the reason that she had to hang up was because there were a few arrangements that needed to be made for her well-deserved vacation.

Many writers pad their writing with wordy phrasing or empty verbiage—and that's a hard habit to break. You may find that you ramble on in your first draft because you're thinking as you write. Or perhaps you want to impress readers with lots of words; but all those words just fill up space without saying anything. Passive voice and nominalizations often lead to wordiness, partly because these weak writing styles force you to use forms of the verb *to be*. You already know how to combat passive writing and weak verbs. Now let's tackle other ways to turn verbose, vague sentences into concise ones that hold your readers' attention.

HOW TO DETECT AND CORRECT WORDY SENTENCES

Wordiness comes in two varieties: wordy phrases and bloated sentence style. The chart below shows some common wordy phrases and their more concise counterparts. The streamlined versions almost always sound better—and they get to the point faster.

WORDY PHRASE	WORDY SENTENCE	HOW TO REWRITE	CONCISE SENTENCE
despite the fact that *even though* *in spite of* *the fact that*	<u>Despite the fact that</u> the counterfeiter was incarcerated, his cronies still circulated fake bills. (14 words)	Use *although* instead.	Although the counterfeiter was incarcerated, his cronies still circulated fake bills. (11 words)
not only … but also	After pursuing the suspect for six miles, the officer was <u>not only</u> exhausted, <u>but he was also</u> embarrassed that he tripped in a pothole. (24 words)	Delete *not only* and *but also*. Use *and* or *as well as* instead.	After pursuing the suspect for six miles, the officer was exhausted and embarrassed that he tripped in a pothole. (19 words)

on a [adjective] *basis*	The part-time dispatcher hoped she could soon work <u>on a full-time basis</u>. (14 words)	Delete *on a* and *basis*. Use the adjective that came before *basis*.	The part-time dispatcher hoped she could soon work full time. (11 words)
in a [adjective] *manner*	The patrollers searched the neighborhood <u>in a thorough manner</u>. (9 words)	Delete *in a* and *manner*. Turn the adjective that came before *manner* into an adverb (usually, by adding *-ly* to the adjective).	The patrollers searched the neighborhood thoroughly. (6 words)
each and every	The warden gave the same pep talk to <u>each and every</u> new inmate. (13 words)	Use either *each* or *every*.	The warden gave the same pep talk to every new inmate. (11 words)

You'll encounter many other wordy phrases. See if you can find other examples in your own writing and elsewhere.

When readers encounter a wordy phrase, they might say to themselves, *That was a bit long-winded*. When entire paragraphs are bloated, readers feel as if they're wading through mud. They struggle to grasp the writer's meaning through all those unnecessary words. Here are three ways to tell you're being verbose.

1. *The sentence may be wordy if it contains a form of the verb* to be. Many wordy paragraphs are filled with forms of this verb: *am, is, are, was, were, be, being, been.* When you limit how often you use *to be* verbs, you automatically write more concisely—and you write better.

Let's look at some common wordy constructions that use forms of *to be.* The concise versions almost always read better. Keep in mind that, in each of these wordy constructions, the form of the verb *to be* may appear in any tense (present, past, or future).

WORDY CONSTRUCTION	WORDY SENTENCE	HOW TO REWRITE	CONCISE SENTENCE
there is ... that *there is ... who*	There were three arson investigators who attended the seminar on how to hide matches from pyromaniacs. (16 words)	Delete *there,* the form of *to be,* and *that* or *who.* Keep everything else.	Three arson investigators attended the seminar on how to hide matches from pyromaniacs. (13 words)

it is … that *this is … that* *that is … that*	It is obvious <u>that</u> neon uniforms would give away cops who wish to surprise suspects at night. (17 words)	Delete this entire construction. Then use the remaining words.	Neon uniforms would give away cops who wish to surprise suspects at night. (13 words)
is able to *are able to*	The police chief hopes his officers <u>are able to</u> nab the mouse that nibbled on his cheese sandwich. (18 words)	Use *can* instead.	The police chief hopes his officers can nab the mouse that nibbled on his cheese sandwich. (16 words)
the reason that … is because	<u>The reason that</u> they didn't detect the explosives <u>was because</u> the bomb-sniffing dog was stuffed up. (17 words)	Delete *the reason that* and the form of *to be*. Keep *because*.	They didn't detect the explosives because the bomb-sniffing dog was stuffed up. (13 words)

You may have noticed that many of the wordy examples here contain the word *that* along with a form of *to be*. The word *that* is often extraneous, so you can usually chop it out when replacing a weak verb.

Your writing automatically becomes clearer and more concise when you eliminate passive voice, nominalizations, and weak verbs. See if you can identify all three weak styles in the passage below.

> **Wordy**
> The cleaning out of the retiring cop's car <u>was</u> a chore <u>that was</u> not looked forward to by the crew <u>that was</u> assigned the job. Not only <u>was there</u> an accumulation of many years' worth of soda cans in the passenger seat, but <u>it was</u> also apparent <u>that</u> Tim's long-haired cat had <u>been</u> allowed to shed all over. (59 words)

To rewrite this paragraph more concisely, look for forms of the verb *to be*. You'll also see that passive voice, nominalizations, and other wordy constructions often tag along. You can significantly shorten the first sentence just by getting rid of the passive voice—making *crew* the subject of the sentence and using an active verb. If you then identify and remove the nominalizations (*the cleaning out of* and *an accumulation of*), you can easily clean up the *to be* verbs and their wordy compatriots.

Concise

The crew did not look forward to cleaning out the retiring cop's car. Many years' worth of soda cans had accumulated in the passenger seat, and Tim's long-haired cat had shed all over. (34 words)

When you're trying to revise a very wordy passage, you may find it difficult to reword everything at once; self-editing is not easy. However, with some practice and frequent review of the chapters in this book, you'll get the hang of it.

2. *The sentence may be wordy if it contains other weak verbs. To be is not the only weak verb. To do, to make,* and *to have* are examples of other weak verbs. When you choose a colorful verb, you can often eliminate wordiness automatically. This chart shows some wordy constructions that contain weak verbs. Their concise counterparts are much clearer.

WORDY CONSTRUCTION	WORDY SENTENCE	HOW TO REWRITE	CONCISE SENTENCE
give [someone or something] *the ability to*	Well-drawn composite sketches give police the ability to close in on suspects. (13 words)	Use *allow* [someone or something] *to* instead.	Well-drawn composite sketches allow police to close in on suspects. (11 words)

have the capability of [doing something]	The seasoned cop claimed he <u>had the capability of</u> arresting one criminal an hour. (14 words)	Use *can* [do something] instead.	The seasoned cop claims he can arrest one criminal an hour. (11 words)
have the effect of [doing something]	The curfew <u>had the effect of</u> reducing crime by 50 percent. (11 words)	Delete *have the effect of* and use the verb that followed *of* in the original.	The curfew reduced crime by 50 percent. (7 words)
serve to [do something]	The shocking crime <u>served to</u> remind homeowners to lock their doors. (11 words)	Delete *serve to* and use the verb that followed *to* in the original.	The shocking crime reminded homeowners to lock their doors. (9 words)

Strong verbs make for concise sentences. Weak verbs often lead to wordy sentences.

3. *A sentence may be wordy because you've inadvertently repeated yourself.* You often try to clarify your ideas as you write, so you may say the same thing twice.

Wordy

The <u>a cappella</u> police chorus entertained the inmates at the minimum-security prison. The <u>singers, who did not have any instruments to back them up,</u> <u>sang</u> three tunes from the 1970s. (31 words)

A cappella means "without instruments," so you can cut a lot out of these two wordy sentences. Here's one sentence that imparts the same information.

Concise

The a cappella police chorus entertained the inmates at the minimum-security prison by singing three tunes from the 1970s. (20 words)

Another often-overlooked repetition involves the use of *and* with *in addition*, *as well as*, or *also*.

Wordy

The judge threw out the forced confession <u>and in addition</u> reprimanded the prosecutor for arriving late.

One word or phrase to indicate *and* is enough.

It's often hard to notice when you're being wordy or repetitious. Problem areas become more obvious if you put your writing aside for a while before rewriting.

WHY YOU SHOULD AVOID WORDY SENTENCES

1. *Wordy writing is often dull and hard to understand.* Bloated writing bores or confuses readers, who can't concentrate on what you're trying to say.

Wordy and uninteresting

<u>The reason that</u> the usefulness of the profiling technique cannot <u>be underestimated</u> <u>is because</u> many criminals can <u>be caught</u> if the authorities know what kind of offender they're looking for. (30 words)

That's a lot of dry verbiage. Readers don't want to spend time figuring out your point, so it's better to state what you mean clearly and quickly.

Much better

Profiling allows police to catch many criminals because the authorities know what kind of offender they're looking for. (18 words)

Imagine page after page of passive voice, nominalizations, and weak verbs. Such prose sounds unpolished—and is often unreadable. Just think of the last legal document you tried to wade through. Lawyers aren't likely to change their incomprehensible writing style, but you can work on yours.

Get in the habit of asking yourself, *Can I say the same thing in fewer words?*

2. *Wordy writing lacks substance.* When you're not sure what to say, you may fill up space with vague, empty writing.

Wordy and vague

<u>It is</u> well known <u>that</u> security cameras <u>are something that</u> can catch criminals in the act. <u>The reason that</u> they <u>are</u> so effective <u>is because</u> clear images <u>are</u> something <u>that</u> can help with the prosecution of robbers in court. (39 words)

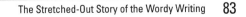

Readers can gather from these two sentences that security cameras fight crime, but you can include twice as much useful information in the same space if you eliminate wordiness and add substance.

Precise and informative
Clear images from security cameras allow businesses to successfully prosecute robbers caught in the act. Police recommend you change the tapes regularly and use high-quality machines that capture all areas of your business. (34 words)

The first sentence sums up in fifteen words what originally took thirty-nine words. To eliminate wordiness as you're writing or rewriting, focus your thoughts and then make every word count.

The best writing teacher I ever had limited us to one-paragraph essays. We had to fit lots of ideas into our paragraph, so we learned to use words sparingly. You can too. Simply distill in your mind the essence of what you want to say, and then state your ideas in simple, clear sentences. You don't need to dress up your thoughts with extra words.

WHEN IT'S OKAY TO BE WORDY

Don't worry about rambling a bit in your rough draft. It's important to get that first flow of ideas down on paper. However, when you're polishing your final version, cut out wordy phrasing and repetition.

RECAP

1. Count the words in a sentence or paragraph. Have you used lots of words but said little?

2. Underline weak and wordy verbs. Look especially for forms of *to be* (*am, is, are, was, were, be, being, been*) and the word *that*.

3. Underline all passive voice, nominalizations, repetitions, and wordy constructions. Keep the essence of your original thought be reword your ideas more concisely.

4. Count the words in the new sentence or paragraph. You should have a lot fewer than before.

WORDY SENTENCES	BETTER SENTENCES
The thing <u>that was</u> suspicious about the man who <u>was</u> loitering next to the fruit stand <u>was that</u> he wore a sign saying, *I like stealing lemons.* (27 words)	The suspicious man loitering next to the fruit stand wore a sign saying, *I like stealing lemons.* (17 words)

The restaurant failed to serve adequately hot coffee, which <u>had the effect of</u> causing one customer to sue the company for emotional trauma. (23 words)	The restaurant's coffee wasn't hot enough, so one customer sued for emotional trauma. (13 words)
The serenader <u>waited around for twenty-four hours</u> for his ex-girl-friend, who finally appeared after he <u>waited a whole day</u>. Then he started <u>not only</u> singing <u>but also</u> playing his guitar <u>as well</u>. (33 words)	The serenader waited twenty-four hours for his ex-girlfriend. When she finally appeared, he started singing and play-ing his guitar. (20 words)

Exercise

It's your turn to detect and correct some wordy sentences. Reread the mystery at the beginning of this chapter, find all the wordy areas, then re-write the story. Appendix two shows the wordy phrases underlined and one way to rewrite the mystery. It's okay if your rewrite and the answer key don't match exactly.

SUMMARY

Bloated writing full of *to be* verbs and wordy phrases will bore your readers. When your sentences are concise instead of wordy, you'll keep your readers' attention as well as save their time.

Appendix One

THE TOP TEN WRITING MISDEMEANORS

Misdemeanor One: Murdering Your Apostrophes 90

Misdemeanor Two: Killing Clichés to Death................. 93

Misdemeanor Three: Committing Fraud
by Confusing Similar-Sounding Words.............94

Misdemeanor Four: Dismembering Your Hyphens........ 95

Misdemeanor Five: Maiming Your Comparisons........... 98

Misdemeanor Six: Grossly Neglecting
Your Subject-Verb Agreement........................... 102

Misdemeanor Seven: Assaulting Your Audience
With Generic Vocabulary 104

Misdemeanor Eight: Brandishing Misplaced
Quotation Marks 105

Misdemeanor Nine: Beating Up Your Pronouns 106

Misdemeanor Ten: Battering *Woman* by
Using It as an Adjective 109

T his book has shown you how to avoid perpetrating seven serious writing crimes, what you might consider felonies. Now let's briefly look at ten misdemeanors you should avoid.

WRITING MISDEMEANOR ONE: MURDERING YOUR APOSTROPHES

Writers frequently put this poor little guy in the wrong place—or leave him out entirely. Examine these frequent apostrophe mistakes.

Unnecessary apostrophes
Lion's, tiger's, and bear's—oh my!

Correct
Lions, tigers, and bears—oh my!

Missing apostrophes
managers special, ladies night, childrens clothing, six months experience

Correct
manager's special, ladies' night, children's clothing, six months' experience (or, six months of experience)

Misplaced apostrophe
The seven police captain's cars went missing during the retreat.

Correct
The seven police captains' cars went missing during the retreat.

Confused apostrophes
Its nice to finally meet a police dog that does not chase it's own tail.

Correct
It's nice to finally meet a police dog that does not chase its own tail.

Now for some rules and regulations. You use an apostrophe in two main ways. First, use an apostrophe to create a contraction, which is a shorter version of one or more words. (Contractions are sometimes considered conversational, so try to avoid them in formal essays.) An apostrophe replaces the missing letter(s) of the original word or words.

it's (a contraction of *it is* or *it has*)
It's time to turn yourself in.

let's (a contraction of *let us*)
Let's rob a convenience store.

they're (a contraction of *they are*)
They're planning to break in tonight.

who's (a contraction of *who is* or *who has*)
Who's going to try this case?

you're (a contraction of *you are*)
You're under arrest!

Second, use an apostrophe to make a noun possessive. A possessive indicates ownership. To make a singular word possessive, add an apostrophe plus *s* after the word: *the detective's cases*. To make a plural word that ends in *s* possessive, add just an apostrophe after the word: *the criminals' hangout*.

When you're forming the possessive of a regular noun, make sure to put the apostrophe in the right place: before the *s* if the noun is singular, and after the *s* if the noun is plural. Many writers misplace apostrophes because they forget the noun is plural: They write *six customer's orders* instead of *six customers' orders*, for instance.

Some possessive adjectives sound like contractions that do use an apostrophe. Be aware, though, that possessive adjectives do not contain an apostrophe.

its
The department had to catch Jack Ripper; its reputation was on the line.

their
They stole from their mom.

whose
"Whose cell should we toss next?" asked the prison guard.

your
Your rap sheet is rather long.

It's a good idea to pay attention to similar-sounding words, especially *it's* and *its*, *they're* and *their*, and *you're* and *your*. When you see one of these easy-to-confuse pairs, spend a few extra seconds to make sure you've chosen the right one. The contraction *it's* and the possessive adjective *its* are often confused—probably because you would expect to form the possessive of *it* by adding an apostrophe and an *s*. If you're prone to using *it's* or *its* incorrectly, underline all instances of these words in your writing and examine each one individually. Whenever you write *it's*, make sure you can substitute either *it is* or *it has* in the sentence.

Never use an apostrophe to form a plural. It's extremely common to see unnecessary apostrophes at the end of nouns. Keep a sharp eye out for this mistake in your own writing.

Incorrect
I sold many <u>sock's</u> at the swap meet.

Correct
I sold many socks at the swap meet.

WRITING MISDEMEANOR TWO: KILLING CLICHÉS TO DEATH

A cliché is any expression that's been used too often, such as *up against the ropes* and *strong as an ox*. When readers encounter phrases they've seen over and over, they don't pay much attention. Inventive ways of putting words together, on the other hand, jump out at readers and make them remember what you've written.

The first person who wrote *think outside the box*, for example, was very creative; these days, though, that phrase no longer impacts readers because its meaning has been so diluted. Understandably, you don't want to reinvent the wheel (another cliché), so you're tempted to use familiar phrases. It's okay to use clichés occasionally; they become a problem only when you use too many.

WRITING MISDEMEANOR THREE: COMMITTING FRAUD BY CONFUSING SIMILAR-SOUNDING WORDS

Writers often mix up words that sound the same or look similar but that have different spellings and meanings. The wrong word may confuse or unintentionally amuse readers.

Incorrect
The officer found herself <u>waste</u> deep in a quagmire; luckily the suspect was stuck in the mud too.

If you read this sentence too quickly, your brain might miss the big mistake (*waste deep* should be *waist deep*). *Waste* means garbage (or worse!); *waist* means an area of the body.

Unfortunately, you can't rely on your word processor's spell-check feature to catch these kinds of mistakes. Spell-checkers point out typos and misspellings, not the incorrect use of a correctly spelled word. It's hard to catch yourself making a mistake with similar-sounding words, so try to reread your writing with a critical eye. And, as always, don't forget to use your dictionary.

Watch out for pairs—or trios—of similar words such as these sound-alikes.

```
affect vs. effect
complement vs. compliment
complementary vs. complimentary
```

You can remember that *compliment* and *complimentary* with an *i* mean to be nice; both use the letter *i*.

```
conscience vs. conscious
desert vs. dessert
everyday vs. every day
```

If you can substitute the word *ordinary*, use *everyday*. If you can substitute *each day*, use *every day*. Many businesses mistakenly use *everyday* in their slogans or on their windows. They probably don't realize they're calling their products average.

```
flair vs. flare
formally vs. formerly
hoard vs. horde
loath vs. loathe
palate vs. palette vs. pallet
personal vs. personnel
perspective vs. prospective
principal vs. principle
```

Prospective is related to the noun *prospect*, which means potential customer or likely candidate. Remember that your *principal* is your *pal*.

WRITING MISDEMEANOR FOUR: DISMEMBERING YOUR HYPHENS

Hyphens may be little, but they can make sentences more readable in a big way. You use a hyphen to join two or more words that work together to describe a noun. Hyphens help readers follow the flow of a sentence because they can quickly tell that these descriptive words are one unit. Two (or more) words joined by hyphens are called a *hyphenated compound*.

Confusing
The <u>lion taunting zookeeper</u> was arrested for animal cruelty.

When readers first come to the word *lion*, they logically think the sentence concerns a lion. However, when they get to the word *zookeeper*, they have to backtrack a bit because the sentence is in fact about a wayward zookeeper. A hyphen between *lion* and *taunting* eliminates this confusion because readers see the two words *lion-taunting* as a single unit.

To hyphenate or not to hyphenate—that is the question. These examples will steer you straight.

Correct
The ninety-nine-year-old man pled guilty.

Correct
The thirty-eight-year-old has been in prison for most of his adult life.

Correct
The officer wrote a forty-two-page report.

Correct
The DA's part-time assistant lost the evidence.

Correct
The nineteenth-century prison needs to be renovated.

Correct
A twenty-foot-high wall separates my house from the world.

Incorrect
The wall that separates my house from the world is <u>twenty-feet-high</u>.

Correct
The wall that separates my house from the world is twenty feet high.

You don't need hyphens if the compound comes after what it describes. In the above example, *twenty feet high* describes *the wall*, which comes earlier in the sentence.

Correct
The museum is exhibiting thirteenth- to seventeenth-century works.

Correct
That textbook works for both low- and high-level students.

When you're using two hyphenated compounds that share a final element, you can omit the final element in the first compound, as in the two examples above: *thirteenth-* and *low-*. You could write *thirteenth-century to seventeenth-century works* or *low-level and high-level students*. However, the abbreviated form eliminates unnecessary repetition. If you omit a shared element in a compound, make sure to put a space after the hyphen in the first item; *low-and high-level students* is incorrect.

Incorrect

The <u>incredibly-fashionable</u> thief left Gucci footprints at the crime scene.

Correct

The incredibly fashionable thief left Gucci footprints at the crime scene.

Don't use a hyphen between an adverb that ends in -*ly* and an adjective. Readers can already tell the adverb and adjective are linked.

Incorrect

The dog <u>snatcher-the</u> one who took my neighbor's <u>puppy-returned</u> the pooch the next day because it bit him.

Correct

The dog snatcher—the one who took my neighbor's puppy—returned pooch the next day because it bit him.

Don't use hyphens instead of em dashes. Short hyphens instead of long em dashes can confuse readers.

WRITING MISDEMEANOR FIVE: MAIMING YOUR COMPARISONS

Comparisons can be tricky. In your mind, you're comparing two of the same item (this apple, that apple; this behavior, that behavior; this moment, that moment), but if you don't correctly identify those items in a sentence, you may wind up comparing two incompatible things. When you see comparison words such as *than*, *like*, *unlike*, *similar*, *different*, *more*, and *less*, be aware that an incorrect comparison may be lurking.

Incorrect
His body language was similar to the previous interrogation.

Readers might understand that you're not really comparing *his body language* to *the previous interrogation*, but it's best to use one of the strategies below to avoid confusion. Here are some ways to ensure you're comparing two compatible things.

1. *Refer back to the first item in the comparison with a pronoun (*it *or* they*)*.

Correct
His body language was similar to what it was during the previous interrogation.

2. *Use* that *or* those *to stand in for the second item.* (This technique results in a more formal-sounding sentence.)

Correct
His body language was similar to that during the previous interrogation.

3. *Reword the sentence to get rid of the comparison problem.* This is often the best option because you can use it to avoid vague comparisons. (The sentence *A is better than B* doesn't communicate much information.) Try being more specific.

Correct
During both interrogations, his body language was defiant.

Here are some tips for correct comparisons.

1. *Make sure you don't accidentally use* then *instead of* than *in a comparison.*

Incorrect
Their uniforms fit better <u>then</u> ours.

Correct
Their uniforms fit better than ours.

2. *Beware of one-sided comparisons.*

Incorrect
The current police chief is <u>more effective</u>.

When readers encounter sentences that are missing the other side of the comparison, they ask, *More effective than who?*

Correct
The current police chief is more effective than his predecessor.

Take any opportunity to make your comparisons more specific.

Even better
The current police chief has brought down more criminals than his predecessor did.

3. *Know when to use* less *and* fewer. You use *less* before adjectives and adverbs. You probably already do so automatically.

Correct
The policeman proved himself less fit than the criminal who outran him.

Correct
The DNA results came back less quickly than she'd hoped.

It's more difficult to know when to use *less* and *fewer* in relation to nouns. Use *less* with uncountable nouns, such as *sand* and *flour*. These nouns are called uncountable because you can't say *three sands* or *eight flours*.

Correct
We have less money in the bank today than we did last week.

Fewer, on the other hand, goes with countable nouns, such as *convicts* and *parolees*. These nouns are countable because you can say *six convicts* or *ninety-nine parolees*.

Correct
Eugene wears fewer tattoos than his cellmate.

Writers often mistakenly use *less* instead of *fewer* before countable nouns.

Incorrect
Eugene wears <u>less tattoos</u> than his cellmate.

In this case, *fewer tattoos* sounds a little fuddy-duddy. If you don't like the way *fewer* reads in your sentence, go ahead and rewrite to avoid the problem.

Correct
Eugene doesn't have as many tattoos as his cellmate.

4. *Make sure to use the correct pronoun after the word* than.

Incorrect
She's more law-abiding <u>than him</u>.

Correct
She's more law-abiding than he.

A quick way to tell whether you're using the wrong pronoun is to add the missing verb at the end. *More law-abiding than him is* obviously sounds wrong. *More law-abiding than he is* sounds right. If you think that the correct pronoun makes the sentence sound a bit stilted, just rewrite the sentence to avoid the problem.

Correct
She hasn't been to jail at all, but he's been locked up twice.

WRITING MISDEMEANOR SIX: GROSSLY NEGLECTING YOUR SUBJECT-VERB AGREEMENT

A singular subject requires a singular verb. A plural subject requires a plural verb. Most of the time it's easy to tell if the subject is singular or plural. *Investigator* is singular. *Investigators* is plural. Two singular subjects joined by *and* combine to make a plural subject: *The investigator and his assistant are accountable.* Two singular subjects joined by *or*, however, take a singular verb: *The investigator or his assistant is accountable.*

Writers invite mistakes with subject-verb agreement when they use subjects that are far from the main verb and subjects with lots of components. Writers are prone to choosing the wrong verb when distracting prepositional phrases or clauses beginning with *that*, *which*, or *who* follow the main word of the subject. In such cases, the main verb is dangerously distant from the subject of the sentence.

Incorrect

The <u>suspect</u> in the stretch limo that crashed into several trailers <u>were taken</u> to the hospital with a concussion.

Here the subject is *suspect*. All the other stuff—*in the stretch limo that crashed into several trailers*—is irrelevant as far as subject-verb agreement is concerned. However, it's easy to get distracted and think you should match the verb to the noun closest to the verb. In this example, *were taken* agrees with *trailers*, but *trailers* isn't the subject. The verb must agree with *suspect*, so you need a singular verb: *was taken*.

When you're checking to make sure your subject agrees with your verb, disregard extra words attached to the main word of the subject. Be especially careful with complicated subjects.

Incorrect

The <u>defendant</u>, who looked stunning in her prison stripes, <u>and her counsel</u>, who nearly tripped in her wobbly heels, <u>was hoping</u> the prosecutor wouldn't show up.

If you ignore the two modifying clauses, *who looked stunning in her prison stripes* and *who nearly tripped in her wobbly heels*, you can see that the subject here is plural: *the defendant... and her counsel*. You should therefore use a plural verb (*were hoping*) instead of a singular one (*was hoping*).

Even if you fix the subject-verb agreement problem, the sentence is still a bit long and hard to follow. Keeping in mind what you learned in chapter six, you can improve the sentence—and avoid the agreement problem—by breaking the sentence into two.

Two shorter sentences
Miss Stealstamps looked stunning in her prison stripes, while Miss Demeanor nearly tripped in her wobbly heels. Both were hoping the prosecutor wouldn't show up.

Consider rewriting your sentence if lots of extra phrases or clauses are attached to the main word of your subject. You can often avoid problems with subject-verb agreement when your subject and verb are near each other.

WRITING MISDEMEANOR SEVEN: ASSAULTING YOUR AUDIENCE WITH GENERIC VOCABULARY

Readers enjoy specific, entertaining prose (writing that's thought provoking, rich in meaning, ironic, comical, attention getting, on target, insightful, and clever). Throughout this book, you've learned many ways to avoid vague and wordy writing and how to replace weak verbs. You know to avoid phrases such as *there is, it is, this is,* and *is able to.*

In the same vein, replace vague nouns and adjectives. You can almost always think of better nouns than *people*, *man*, and *thing*, which are usually too general. Adjectives such as *good*, *interesting*, and *different* are neither good nor interesting to read.

Vary your vocabulary when you can. Try not to repeat the same word in a sentence or paragraph (excepting indispensable words like *the*, *to*, etc.). However, to avoid attracting negative attention to your work, don't use pompous-sounding or out-of-place vocabulary.

WRITING MISDEMEANOR EIGHT: BRANDISHING MISPLACED QUOTATION MARKS

You generally use quotation marks to quote exactly what someone said or wrote, or to indicate dialogue. You can also use quotation marks around a word or expression to let readers know you're being deceitful or sarcastic.

Correct
The policeman "searched" the house because his superior told him to. He knew the owner, his best friend, couldn't be hiding a weapon, so he just pretended to look around.

However, writers often incorrectly put something in quotation marks to add emphasis.

Incorrect
At the fire department's open house this weekend, you can fill up on some "free" tamales.

If you write *"free" tamales*, you're actually implying that they're not free. Use italics to emphasize a word or expression, or reword the sentence to highlight your point.

You can tell that you've incorrectly used quotation marks to highlight something if you engage in a little pantomime. Imagine yourself making the quotation mark sign with your fingers as you're saying the sentence out loud. If what's in quotation marks can be construed as sarcastic or deceitful, then your quotation marks can stay. If not, find some other way to emphasize what you want to say.

WRITING MISDEMEANOR NINE: BEATING UP YOUR PRONOUNS

A noun is a person, place, or thing. A pronoun stands in for a noun that has already been mentioned or implied: The victim cried when *she* spotted the man at the grocery store. A pronoun also can refer back to another pronoun: The victim cried when *she* spotted *her* assailant. Common pronouns include *he*, *she*, *him*, *her*, and *they*. The word that a pronoun stands in for is called an *antecedent*.

When you use a pronoun to refer back to a noun or another pronoun, you need to make sure the antecedent and pronoun match up—both must be singular, or both must be plural. It's easy to make the antecedent (*gangster*) and pronoun (*his*) agree in this sentence.

Correct
When the gangster dropped off his white suit at the cleaner's, the clerk knew not to point out the reddish stains.

Writers often mistakenly use the plural pronouns *they, their,* and *them* when referring back to a singular antecedent. You may find yourself using a plural pronoun when you don't know the gender of the person you're writing about.

Incorrect
The <u>witness</u> looked carefully at the men in the lineup and pointed to the one <u>they</u> saw rob the diner.

Here the plural pronoun *they* refers to the singular noun *witness*. This could confuse readers, who might think that *they* refers back to *men*. If you know the gender of a singular antecedent, use *he, she,* or *it,* whichever is appropriate. If the witness is a woman, for example, you should use *she* instead of *they*.

If you don't know the gender of the antecedent, choose one of the techniques below to eliminate pronoun-antecedent disagreement. (Not all of these strategies will work in every case. Pick the one that best fits the situation.)

1. Repeat the antecedent instead of using a pronoun.

2. Choose to use either a masculine or a feminine pronoun (*he* or *she, him* or *her, his* or *her*) and then use that pronoun consistently throughout the document.

3. Use the phrase *he or she*, *him or her*, or *his or her* instead of just *he* or just *she*. Note that this technique may annoy readers if you overuse it.

4. Pluralize the antecedent. Then use *they*, *their*, or *them* when you refer back to the original noun.

5. Rewrite the sentence to avoid the problem altogether. This strategy, as well as number four above, is often the best way to avoid a problem with pronoun-antecedent agreement.

Be especially careful when you use indefinite pronouns as antecedents. Indefinite pronouns include *everyone*, *somebody*, and *no one*.

Incorrect
Everybody thinks their children can do no wrong.

In this sentence, the antecedent of the pronoun *their* is the singular indefinite pronoun *everybody*. *Their* and *everybody* don't match. In everyday speech, you'll often hear people using the pronoun *their* to correspond with *everybody*. In writing, though, you must be more exact. Use one of the five techniques listed above to fix the agreement problem. In this case, the best way to fix this mistake is probably to change *everybody* (singular) to a plural.

Correct
All parents think their children can do no wrong.

Correct
Most people think their children can do no wrong.

WRITING MISDEMEANOR TEN:
BATTERING *WOMAN* BY USING IT AS AN ADJECTIVE

All editors encounter pet peeves—errors that bother them more than other mistakes. Here's one of mine: I'd like to discourage you from using *woman* and *women* as adjectives, as in *woman firefighter* or *woman author*. *Woman* and *man* are nouns. You wouldn't say *man nurse* (*male nurse* is common lingo), so it shouldn't be much of a stretch to say *female firefighter* or *female author*. If you don't like how that sounds, just reword the sentence. Instead of writing *I admire women firefighters*, try *I admire women who work as firefighters*.

Appendix Two

ANSWER KEY

CHAPTER ONE

The pile of case files <u>was carefully laid out</u> as Detective Pinkersolve decided which one <u>should be tackled</u> first.

A puzzling caper at the local museum of modern art needed <u>to be solved</u> quickly, so the facts <u>were examined by</u> her. Last night, everything <u>was being prepared</u> for opening day of the much-<u>anticipated</u> exhibition of self-portraits. It <u>was discovered by</u> the cleaning crew that one painting <u>had been defaced</u>. When the crime scene <u>was studied closely by</u> the detective, it <u>was revealed</u> that a portrait of a man <u>had been scribbled on</u> with red crayon. It <u>was decided</u> a visit needed <u>to be paid</u> to the man whose self-portrait <u>had been given</u> a mustache.

When the artist <u>was interviewed</u>, it <u>was noted</u> that his scruffy red mustache was the same as the one <u>depicted by</u> the self-portrait. When <u>confronted</u>, the artist explained that his painting had not been ready at the deadline, so the museum <u>had been snuck into</u> and some last-minute touches <u>added</u>. Although an apology <u>was issued</u> and a fine <u>paid</u>, bad press <u>could not be avoided</u>. Artistic success

<u>was never achieved</u>, so career options <u>were evaluated</u>. A few ideas <u>were suggested</u> and the case file <u>closed</u>.

Detective Pinkersolve carefully laid out her pile of case files and decided which one to tackle first.

She needed to quickly solve a puzzling caper at the local museum of modern art, so she examined the facts. Last night, everything was being prepared for opening day of the much-anticipated exhibition of self-portraits. The cleaning crew discovered that one painting had been defaced. When the detective studied the crime scene closely, she saw that a portrait of a man had been scribbled on with red crayon. She decided to pay a visit to the man whose self-portrait now wore a mustache.

When Detective Pinkersolve interviewed the artist, she noted that his scruffy red mustache was the same as the one in the self-portrait. When she confronted the artist, he explained that his painting had not been ready at the deadline, so he snuck into the museum and added some last-minute touches. Although he apologized and paid a fine, he couldn't avoid all the bad press. He never achieved artistic success, so he had to evaluate his career options. Detective Pinkersolve suggested a few ideas and then closed the case file.

Note: Some passive voice has been left here; you shouldn't automatically change every passive construction.

CHAPTER TWO

Detective Pinkersolve was ready for <u>the selection of</u> her next case. <u>The decision</u> to study Miss Crustlepuff's file was made because this might be her only opportunity to see the spinster's opulent villa.

<u>An examination of</u> the facts revealed a mystery whose <u>solution</u> could be reached only through superb <u>detecting</u>. <u>Astonishment</u> by Miss Crustlepuff had occurred upon <u>the realization</u> that a thief had absconded with her TV and toaster. However, the perpetrator's <u>leaving of</u> the heirloom silverware caused much <u>head scratching</u>. After <u>a look-around of</u> the grounds, the spinster puzzled over the two huge footprints near the service entrance.

Following <u>a conversation</u> with Miss Crustlepuff, Detective Pinkersolve felt <u>confidence</u> the case was nearing <u>completion</u>. The spinster knew only one person with enormous feet: a recently let-go employee. <u>The questioning of</u> the ex-maid revealed that she had wanted to pawn the silver, but its <u>heaviness</u> prevented <u>removal</u>. <u>The carrying off of</u> the small TV and extremely light toaster happened instead. She claimed the <u>theft</u> was necessary because she needed money for <u>the purchase of</u> some extra-large shoes. Although the items were returned, the ex-maid learned true <u>repentance</u> only after spending time in jail.

Detective Pinkersolve was ready to select her next case. She decided to study Miss Crustlepuff's file because this might be her only opportunity to see the spinster's opulent villa.

The facts she examined revealed a mystery that only a superb detective could solve. An astonished Miss Crustlepuff had realized that a thief had absconded with her TV and toaster. However, she didn't understand why the perpetrator had left the heirloom silverware. After the spinster looked around the grounds, she puzzled over the two huge footprints near the service entrance.

After Detective Pinkersolve spoke with Miss Crustlepuff, the detective felt confident she would close the case soon. The spinster knew only one person with enormous feet: a recently let-go employee. When the detective questioned the ex-maid, she learned that the maid had wanted to pawn the silver, but it was too heavy to remove. Instead, she carried off the small TV and extremely light toaster. She claimed she had to steal from Miss Crustlepuff because she needed money to purchase some extra-large shoes. Although the ex-maid returned the items, she became truly repentant only after spending time in jail.

CHAPTER THREE

Something stood out immediately <u>while leafing through</u> the stack of cases. "Oh, poor Monsieur Gourmand," sympathized Detective Pinkersolve.

<u>Solving</u> this assault with a dessert fork was a priority because <u>snacking</u> on éclairs from Monsieur Gourmand's patisserie, Le Chocolate Moose, was enjoyable <u>when not working</u>. <u>Questioning</u> the witness led to information that the crime occurred <u>while preparing</u> some chocolate-filled delights. Two vital clues were then uncovered <u>when pointing out</u> an abandoned razor near the scene and <u>hinting</u> that the new waiter might be involved.

Next up was <u>interviewing</u> Mr. Goostache, the unkempt waiter. <u>Arguing</u> with Monsieur Gourmand over his appearance had caused Mr. Goostache to defend his crumb-filled facial hair <u>when seeing</u> a razor in his hand. <u>Stabbing</u> his boss wasn't intended, but <u>shaving</u> wasn't an option. Perhaps <u>combing</u> his moustache better <u>when next getting</u> ready for work would be a good idea.

<u>Closing</u> the case was accomplished <u>after giving</u> the detective a free éclair and <u>deciding</u> not to file charges. <u>Finding</u> another waiter who could speak with a fake French accent wouldn't be easy. Her work here was done <u>after thanking</u> Monsieur Gourmand for the opportunity to serve—and to eat.

Something stood out immediately as Detective Pinker-solve leafed through the stack of cases. "Oh, poor Monsieur Gourmand," she sympathized.

The detective made it a priority to find out who had assaulted Monsieur Gourmand with a dessert fork because she enjoyed snacking on éclairs from his patisserie, Le Chocolate Moose. She questioned a witness and learned that the crime occurred while Monsieur Gourmand was preparing some chocolate-filled delights. She uncovered two vital clues when her witness pointed out an abandoned razor near the scene and hinted that the new waiter might be involved.

She next interviewed Mr. Goostache, the unkempt waiter. Mr. Goostache and Monsieur Gourmand had argued over the waiter's appearance. When Mr. Goostache saw his boss wielding a razor, he had defended himself and his crumb-filled facial hair. The waiter declared he hadn't intended to stab Monsieur Gourmand, but he refused to be shaved. The detective suggested he comb his moustache better the next time he got ready for work.

Detective Pinkersolve had closed the case. Monsieur Gourmand gave her a free éclair and explained he'd decided not to file charges. He didn't think he could find another waiter who could speak with a fake French accent. The detective thanked Monsieur Gourmand for the opportunity to serve—and to eat—and then bade him farewell.

CHAPTER FOUR

Detective Pinkersolve's next case involved a man who may have been poisoned. His gastric symptoms <u>got</u> better, but he didn't know what <u>had made</u> him ill. <u>There were</u> no unusual chemicals lying about the house. He hoped <u>it wasn't</u> arsenic poisoning.

He thought <u>it was</u> possible his new dog walker <u>was</u> guilty because they had recently argued. Apparently Miss Poodlepull didn't <u>want</u> to walk Pookie around the block ten times. <u>It was</u> tiring, so she <u>went</u> around only eight times. When Detective Pinkersolve talked with Miss Poodlepull, <u>it was</u> clear she <u>was</u> too busy to poison anyone. <u>There were</u> nine dogs for her to walk each day.

<u>It was</u> time to close the case. <u>There were</u> some questions asked and some revealing answers given. The detective learned that the man's grandson, a student at the culinary institute, had recently cooked some meals for him. <u>It was</u> certain that a new recipe from Sonny's oyster class had caused the stomach pains. Sonny <u>was</u> very sorry. He offered to <u>make</u> the two of them a special meal to make up for all the trouble. Both quickly said that <u>there were</u> other things they <u>had</u> to <u>do</u>. <u>It was</u> time for Detective Pinkersolve to move on to her next case.

Detective Pinkersolve's next case involved a man who may have been poisoned. He bounced back quickly but wondered what had doubled him over. He didn't keep any unusual chemicals around the house, and he hoped it wasn't arsenic poisoning.

Maybe his new dog walker had tried to do him in. He suspected her because they had recently argued. Apparently Miss Poodlepull refused to walk Pookie around the block ten times. Her legs got too tired, so she traipsed around only eight times. Detective Pinkersolve cleared the suspect after they talked. Miss Poodlepull was too busy to poison anyone; she had to walk nine dogs each day.

Detective Pinkersolve solved the case when she asked some questions and heard some revealing answers. She learned that the man's grandson, a student at the culinary institute, had recently cooked some meals for him. She deduced that a new recipe from Sonny's oyster class had caused the stomach pains. Sonny apologized for all the trouble and offered to whip up a special meal for them. They quickly declined, citing previous commitments. Detective Pinkersolve, for one, had to move on to her next case.

CHAPTER FIVE

Gazing outside, it occurred to Detective Pinkersolve that she was nearly done with her cases. Off to interview a witness from a recent carjacking caper, there was no time to lose.

The witness had seen a man trying to carjack a woman brandishing a weapon. Looking around for another vehicle because he couldn't drive a stick shift, a pizza delivery bike soon came by that sported a Slow Poke Pizza sign. While munching on a cold slice, police put out an APB for a man with an anchovy on his face who was cycling slowly.

Upset that the culprit got away, a wanted poster was drawn that Detective Pinkersolve hoped would help capture him. The detective needed to think about the case, so she ordered some pizza from Slow Poke's that would undoubtedly be delicious. After waiting two hours, the pizza finally came. Something struck her that was odd. Jack, the delivery cyclist, looked just like the composite sketch of the bike-jacker! Admitting he was the suspect, jail was avoided. Explaining how, Slow Poke's generous manager was allowing Jack to work off his debt to society. Detective Pinkersolve decided to withhold a tip and began working her next case.

Gazing outside, Detective Pinkersolve realized she was nearly done with her cases. Off to interview a witness from a recent carjacking caper, she had no time to lose.

The witness had seen a man brandishing a weapon as he tried to carjack a woman. The carjacker couldn't drive a stick shift, so he looked around for another vehicle. Just then, a delivery bike that sported a Slow Poke Pizza sign came by. The bike-jacker rode off as he munched on a cold slice. Meanwhile, police put out an APB for a slowly cycling suspect with an anchovy on his face.

Upset that the culprit got away, Detective Pinkersolve hoped a wanted poster would help her capture him. The detective needed to think about the case, so she ordered some pizza from Slow Poke's. It would undoubtedly be delicious. After she waited two hours, the pizza finally came. Something odd struck her. Jack, the delivery cyclist, looked just like the composite sketch of the bike-jacker! He admitted he was the suspect and explained how he had avoided jail. Apparently, Slow Poke's generous manager was allowing Jack to work off his debt to society. Detective Pinkersolve decided to withhold a tip and began working her next case.

CHAPTER SIX

Detective Pinkersolve's next case involved identity theft, a fast-growing crime that was often hard to solve, <u>and</u> it bothered her—all crimes bothered her, actually, <u>but</u> this particular crime causes a huge hassle for its victims, <u>who</u> have to spend a long time straightening things out—<u>because</u> her neighbor (<u>who</u> was a florist) had been targeted.

<u>When</u> Miss Tuliptoes opened the mail, she discovered an astronomical credit card bill (she'd lost the card, along with some potting soil, just last week), <u>and</u> she needed the detective's help—living next to a detective sure was great! Credit 'R Us told the florist she wasn't responsible for the fraudulent charges—<u>boy</u>, was she relieved, <u>since</u> she was strapped for cash—<u>and</u> the detective promised to get on the case right away, <u>but</u> Miss Tuliptoes was actually glad someone had stolen her identity <u>because</u> she was tired of her name (she'd always wanted to change it, <u>and</u> this was the opportunity she'd been looking for). She didn't really want the detective to investigate, she admitted—she just wanted help picking a new name—<u>and</u> so they spent the morning testing out names until Detective Pinkersolve told whatever-her-name-was that she had to look into her next case.

Detective Pinkersolve's next case involved identity theft, a fast-growing crime that was often hard to solve. This particular crime bothered her because her neighbor, a florist, had been targeted. All crimes bothered her, actually, but this crime causes a huge hassle for its victims, who have to spend a long time straightening things out.

When Miss Tuliptoes opened the mail, she discovered an astronomical credit card bill, and she needed the detective's help. After exclaiming that living next to a detective sure was great, she explained she'd lost the card, along with some potting soil, just last week. Credit 'R Us told the florist she wasn't responsible for the fraudulent charges—boy, was she relieved, since she was strapped for cash. The detective promised to get on the case right away, but Miss Tuliptoes was actually glad someone had stolen her identity. Apparently, she was tired of her name. She'd always wanted to change it, and this was the opportunity she'd been looking for. She didn't really want the detective to investigate, she admitted. She just wanted help picking a new name. And so they spent the morning testing out names until Detective Pinkersolve told whatever-her-name-was that she had to look into her next case.

CHAPTER SEVEN

Detective Pinkersolve's last case <u>was one that</u> dealt with graffiti. <u>There had been</u> numerous sightings by the townspeople of spray-paintings of scary dragons exhaling a phone number. The alarming thought <u>that</u> crossed the detective's mind <u>was that there was</u> a new gang <u>that was</u> recruiting <u>new</u> members with these dragons.

When the phone number <u>was called</u>, a mint company <u>was reached</u>. The receptionist's announcement <u>was that this was</u> the first call that <u>had been received</u> by the company. Detective Pinkersolve <u>would therefore be</u> the recipient of a free sample of the company's new Dragon Breath Mints. The explanation <u>was that there was</u> a new mint in town, not a new gang. <u>It was explained that</u> some local art students <u>had been commissioned</u> to advertise these new mints. However, the receptionist's explanation <u>was that</u> the company would have <u>to do</u> a reevaluation of this apparently unsuccessful campaign. The removal of all dragons <u>would be done</u> immediately. Detective Pinkersolve said she felt sure <u>that</u> the company <u>had the capability of</u> thinking of another advertising strategy. She then said <u>the reason that</u> she had to hang up <u>was because there were</u> a few arrangements <u>that</u> needed <u>to be made</u> for her well-deserved vacation.

Detective Pinkersolve's last case dealt with graffiti. The townspeople had seen numerous spray-paintings of scary dragons exhaling a phone number. The alarmed detective worried that a new gang was using these dragons to recruit members in her town.

When the detective called the number, she was surprised to reach a mint company. The receptionist told the detective she was the first person to call, so she would receive a free sample of the company's new Dragon Breath Mints. A new mint—not a new gang—was in town. The receptionist explained that the company had commissioned some local art students to advertise the mints. However, Marketing would have to reevaluate this apparently unsuccessful campaign, and Environmental Services would immediately remove all the dragons. Detective Pinkersolve said she felt sure the company could think of another advertising strategy. She then explained she had to hang up because she needed to make a few arrangements for her well-deserved vacation.

Appendix Three
GLOSSARY

active sentence—A sentence in which the subject, not the object, is performing the action: **The batter struck the ball.** (*The batter* is the subject; *the ball* is the object.) *See also*: object, subject. *Contrast with*: passive sentence.

active voice—*See*: active sentence.

adjective—A word that describes a noun: **happy**. *See also*: noun.

adverb—A word that describes an adjective, a verb, or another adverb: **very** good, I ate **greedily**. *See also*: adjective, verb.

antecedent—The word that a pronoun stands in for: **The man** ate his lunch. *See also*: pronoun.

apostrophe—A punctuation mark (') used to form contractions or to indicate possession: **It's** time to go (it is time to go), one **boy's** shoes, three **boys'** shoes. *See also*: contraction, possessive.

clause—A group of words that often begins with *that*, *who*, or *which*. Contains a subject and a main verb. Is more complex than a phrase: The dog **that I saw at the pet shop** was cute. *See also*: main verb, subject. *Contrast with*: phrase.

cliché—An expression that has been used too often: **larger than life**.

colon—A punctuation mark used to introduce something, especially a list: You need to buy the following pastries: éclairs, hot-cross buns, and pecan tarts.

comma—A punctuation mark used to separate items within a series or within a sentence: They enjoy movies, concerts, operas, and plays.

complete sentence—A sentence that contains a subject and a verb and sometimes an object: **She likes him.** *See also*: object, subject, verb. *Contrast with*: fragment, incomplete sentence.

contraction—A shorter version of one or more words. Use an apostrophe instead of the missing letter(s): **they've** (they have), **it's** (it is, it has). *See also*: apostrophe.

countable noun—A noun you can count: **trees**. *See also*: noun. *Contrast with*: uncountable noun.

em dash—A punctuation mark used to mark an aside: He asked me—me, of all people—to cook his dinner.

exclamation point—A punctuation mark used to express excitement or surprise: I love you!

fragment—A sentence that is missing one of its required parts (a subject, verb, or object). Also known as an incomplete sentence: **She likes.** *See also*: object, subject, verb. *Contrast with*: complete sentence.

hyphen—A punctuation mark used to join related words: The **sixteen-year-old** boy crashed his car.

hyphenated compound—Two (or more) words joined by hyphens: my **chocolate-loving** sister. *See also*: hyphen.

incomplete sentence—*See*: fragment.

indefinite pronoun—A pronoun such as *everyone*, *somebody*, or *no one*. *See also*: pronoun.

main verb—Officially known as a *predicate*, the verb that goes with the subject of the sentence: She **goes** to school. *See also*: subject, verb.

misplaced modifier—A modifier that ends up next to the wrong word: **Looking out the window**, it was clear to me that it was raining. *See also*: modifier.

modifier—A word or short phrase that describes something. Should be right next to what it describes: **Looking out the window**, I saw it was raining.

nominalization—A noun you've created from a verb or an adjective: **recommendation** (from the verb *to recommend*). *See also*: adjective, noun, verb.

noun—A person, place, or thing: **essay, Tom**.

object—The person or thing that receives the action of the verb in a sentence: The batter struck **the ball**. *See also*: active sentence, passive sentence, verb. *Contrast with*: subject.

parallel sentence—A sentence in which all the elements are in the same form: She ran **up the hill, into the woods,** and **down to the lake**. *See also*: base word. *Contrast with*: unparallel sentence.

parentheses—A punctuation mark used to mark incidental information: I put on my raincoat (it was sprinkling).

passive sentence—A sentence in which the recipient of the verb's action is the subject instead of the object: **The ball was struck by the batter.** *See also*: object, subject, verb. *Contrast with*: active sentence.

passive voice—*See*: passive sentence.

past participle—A past-tense form of a verb that appears in passive voice: It was **done** by me. *See also*: passive sentence, verb.

past tense—A form of a verb that indicates something has already happened: I **ate** it. *See also*: verb. *Contrast with*: present tense.

period—A punctuation mark used to end a sentence.

phrase—A short group of words that does not contain both a subject and a main verb. Is less complex than a clause: The dog that I saw **at the pet shop** was cute. *Contrast with*: main verb, subject. *See also*: clause.

plural—More than one item or person: **the books, they.** *Contrast with*: singular.

possessive—A form of a word that denotes ownership or possession: the **boy's** shoes (the shoes that belong to the boy).

preposition—A word that often describes the position of something: **in** the park, **next to** my sister.

prepositional phrase—A phrase that starts with a preposition: **in the park, next to my sister.** *See also*: preposition.

present tense—A form of a verb that indicates something is happening now or happens habitually: They **like** spaghetti. *See also*: verb. *Contrast with*: past tense.

pronoun—A word that takes the place of a noun or another pronoun: **he, they, it**. *See also*: noun.

pronoun-antecedent agreement—When a singular pronoun agrees with a singular antecedent, and a plural pronoun agrees with a plural antecedent: **My aunt** visited **her** cousin. *See also*: antecedent, noun, plural, pronoun, singular.

question mark—A punctuation mark used at the end of a question: Where did I put my keys**?**

quotation mark—A punctuation mark used to indicate a quotation or dialogue, or to signal deceit or sarcasm: She asked, **"**Where did I put my keys?**"**

run-on sentence—An incorrect sentence made up of two sentences joined with a comma instead of a period or semicolon: **I like ice cream, it's good.** *See also*: comma, period, semicolon.

semicolon—A punctuation mark used to separate items that contain commas, or to join two connected sentences into one: I couldn't find my shoes in the closet; however, I did find an old pizza. *See also*: comma.

sentence structure—The way you build your sentence. This book favors active as opposed to passive sentence structure. *See also:* active sentence, passive sentence.

singular—A single item or person: **the book, he**. *Contrast with*: plural.

subject—The person or thing that performs the action of the verb in a sentence: **The batter** struck the ball. *See also*: active sentence, passive sentence, verb. *Contrast with*: object.

subject-verb agreement—When a singular subject agrees with a singular verb, and when a plural subject agrees with a plural verb: **The detective's shoes**, which **are** always pristine, **looked** dirty yesterday. *See also*: plural, singular, subject, verb.

uncountable noun—A noun you can't count: **sand**. *See also*: noun. *Contrast with*: countable noun.

unparallel sentence—A sentence in which similar elements are not in the same form: They like **to fish, barbecuing** their catches, and **to relax** with a beer. *Contrast with*: parallel sentence.

vague *-ing* word—A word ending in *-ing* that allows you to write vaguely or passively. (Not all words ending in *-ing* are vague.) Often leads to a misplaced modifier: After **going** to bed, some barking dogs were noisy. *See also*: misplaced modifier, passive sentence, verb.

verb—A part of speech that indicates the action in a sentence: They **ran** all the way home.

weak verb—A verb that is repetitive, passive, wordy, or general; has multiple meanings; fails to clarify the action; or makes readers work too hard: **to be, to do, to have**. *See also*: passive sentence, verb.

WEAK WRITING RAP SHEET

PROBLEM AREA	WHAT TO LOOK FOR	EXAMPLES
Passive Voice	1. A form of *to be*. 2. A past participle. 3. The word *by*.	• The show <u>was held by</u> the museum. • The carpets <u>were chewed up</u>.
Nominal-izations, or Empty Nouns	1. A word such as *a, an, the, his, her, these,* or *several*. 2. A noun such as *utilization, sadness,* or *taking*. 3. The word *of*.	• I was unsure who had done <u>the beautiful arrangement of</u> flowers. • <u>The cooking of</u> the six-course meal was time consuming.
Pronoun-Antecedent Agreement	Singular antecedent but plural pronoun, or vice versa.	• <u>The detective</u> and <u>their</u> boss…
Woman instead of *Female*	Using *woman* or *women* as an adjective.	• The <u>woman</u> painter became famous.

HOW TO CORRECT IT	BETTER WRITING STYLE
Identify who is doing the action (subject) and who is receiving it (object). Decide if you want to focus on the subject or the object. If the subject is most important, use active voice. Ensure the person/thing doing the action is the subject of the sentence.	• The museum held the show. • The dog chewed up the carpets.
Figure out what verb or adjective to use instead of the nominalization. For example, *a preparation of* becomes the verb *to prepare*, and *the sadness of* becomes the adjective *sad*. Use this verb or adjective when you rewrite. You may need a new subject, so be sure to specify who or what is doing the action.	• I was unsure who had arranged the flowers so beautifully. • The chef spent hours cooking the six-course meal.
If the antecedent is singular, use a singular pronoun. If it's plural, use a plural pronoun.	• The detective and her boss…
Use the word *female* or reword the sentence.	• The female painter became famous.

PROBLEM AREA	WHAT TO LOOK FOR	EXAMPLES
Vague -*ing* Words	A word ending in -*ing*. Appears anywhere in a sentence, especially the first word or after one of these words or phrases: *after, although, before, by, due to, if, instead of, since, though, through, upon, when, whereas,* and *while.*	• <u>Rewriting</u> is fun. • The curtains were drawn before <u>going out</u>.
Weak Verbs	Basic verbs such as *to be, to do, to get, to go, to have, to make, to occur,* and *to use.* Weak phrasing such as *there is, it is,* and *this is.*	• That <u>is</u> a good movie. • He <u>went up</u> the mountain with difficulty.
Misplaced Modifiers	A descriptive phrase that's next to the wrong subject. If at the beginning of a sentence, a phrase followed by a comma. If in the middle/at the end, a *that* or *who* clause.	• <u>Flying around the room</u>, I saw the bird. • I drove over a bug in the driveway <u>that was huge</u>.

HOW TO CORRECT IT	BETTER WRITING STYLE
Determine which sentences with *-ing* words are missing a clear subject. Rewrite each sentence and state who is doing the action. You can often use the verb that appears in the vague *-ing* construction (for example, turn *after going* into *after he goes*). Try to use a more interesting verb than *was* or *were*.	• She enjoys rewriting. • He drew the curtains before they went out.
Use specific, descriptive verbs.	• That movie bowled me over. • He struggled to reach the summit.
Ensure the modifier is right next to what it describes.	• I saw the bird flying around the room. • I drove over a huge bug in the driveway.

PROBLEM AREA	WHAT TO LOOK FOR	EXAMPLES
Long Sentences	More than forty words. Words such as *and, but, after, although, because, before, if, since, so, though, when, which*, and *who*. Pairs of em dashes or parentheses.	• Instead of confessing to the heist, <u>which</u> they took part in yesterday (they robbed a bank with an accomplice), the evil duo, <u>who</u> would no longer have to flip burgers, celebrated.
Wordiness	Many words but little substance. Forms of weak verbs such as *to be*. Passive writing. Phrasing such as *there is ... that* and *the reason is because*. Repetitions of the same idea.	• <u>The utilization of</u> spam <u>by</u> the salesman <u>was</u> why <u>there was</u> lots of money flowing into his bank account. (19 words) • <u>The reason that</u> the policeman was standing in the middle of the road <u>was because</u> the traffic light was not working. (21 words)
Generic Vocabulary	Using overly general nouns, verbs, and adjectives.	• The <u>bad</u> criminal <u>took a lot</u> from my neighbor.
Quotation Marks	Using quotation marks to emphasize something.	• I love you "<u>so much.</u>"

HOW TO CORRECT IT	BETTER WRITING STYLE
Figure out the sentence's main idea and use that as the basis for the primary sentence. Then reroute the other parts of the overly long sentence. The new sentences should flow well together. Transitions should be smooth.	• The evil duo, along with an accomplice, robbed a bank yesterday. Instead of confessing, they celebrated that they would no longer have to flip burgers.
Rewrite most weak verbs. Replace wordy phrases with concise ones. Cut repetitions.	• The spammer got rich. (4 words) • The policeman directed traffic when the signal broke. (8 words)
Use specific words instead of vague ones.	• The law-breaker made off with my neighbor's silverware and credit cards.
Use quotation marks to indicate deceit or sarcasm, not to highlight something. Use italics or reword the sentence if you want to emphasize something.	• I love you so much!

PROBLEM AREA	WHAT TO LOOK FOR	EXAMPLES
Apostrophes	Using *it's* instead of *its* or confusing other pairs of contractions/ possessive adjectives. Using an apostrophe incorrectly with plural nouns. Adding an unneeded apostrophe, such as in a plural noun. Leaving out a needed apostrophe.	• <u>There</u> here. • My <u>childrens'</u> smiles are precious. • These <u>car's</u> are new. • The <u>managers</u> special is fried eggs and bacon.
Clichés	Overusing common phrases.	• The robber <u>gave</u> the policewoman a <u>run for her money</u>.
Hyphens	Forgetting to use hyphens to join related words. Using hyphens if descriptive words come after the noun. Using a hyphen after *-ly* adverbs. Joining too many words with hyphens. Using hyphens instead of em dashes.	• Her <u>wonderfully-talented</u> <u>nineteen year old</u> sister is <u>big-hearted</u>. • The <u>open-the-door-and-call-me-a-taxi</u> doorman went missing. • He passed the <u>polygraph-what</u> a surprise!

HOW TO CORRECT IT	BETTER WRITING STYLE
Be careful to distinguish between contractions (apostrophe) and possessive adjectives (no apostrophe). When you're making a noun possessive, ensure you put the apostrophe in the right place.	• They're here. • My children's smiles are precious. • These cars are new. • The manager's special is fried eggs and bacon.
Pepper your writing with original phrasing.	• The robber evaded the policewoman for a while, but she finally caught him.
Use hyphens to join related words before a noun. Don't use hyphens if these words come after the noun or if you're joining an -ly adverb. Don't confuse readers by joining up too many words with hyphens. Don't use hyphens instead of em dashes.	• Her wonderfully talented nineteen-year-old sister is big hearted. • The doorman, who always opened the door and called a taxi for me, went missing. • He passed the polygraph—what a surprise!

PROBLEM AREA	WHAT TO LOOK FOR	EXAMPLES
Comparisons	Comparing two in-compatible ideas.	• The detective's <u>shoes</u> were newer than his <u>boss</u>.
Subject-Verb Agreement	Singular subject but plural verb, or vice versa.	• The detectives and their boss <u>likes</u> to arrest criminals.
Similar-Sounding Words	Mixing up words that sound the same or look similar but that have different spell-ings and meanings.	• She was <u>loathe</u> to turn herself in.

HOW TO CORRECT IT	BETTER WRITING STYLE
Make sure you're comparing apples to apples.	• The detective's shoes were newer than those of his boss.
Isolate the subject and determine if it's singular or plural. If the subject is singular, use a singular verb. If it's plural, use a plural verb. Plural subjects often contain the word *and*. Consider moving the subject close to the verb.	• The detectives and their boss like to arrest criminals.
Check your dictionary to make sure you're using the word you intend.	• She was loath to turn herself in.

INDEX

A

able to
in wordy constructions, 78, 104

active sentences
defined, 124
See also active voice; passive voice

active voice, 1, 10–14, 16, 17
defined, 124
See also passive voice

adjectives, 48, 124
defined, 124
forming, from nominaliztions, 26, 133
hyphenation of *-ly* adverbs before, 98, 138
less used with, 100
vague, 104
in wordy constructions, 76

adverbs
correcting wordiness with, 76
defined, 124
forming, from adjectives, 76
less used with, 100
-ly, hyphenation after, 98, 138

after
as used with misplaced modifiers, 49–50
in overly long sentences, 63, 68, 136

as used with vague *-ing* words and, 32, 36, 134

allow … to
in wordy constructions, 80

also
in wordy constructions, 82

although
correcting wordiness with, 75
as used with misplaced modifiers, 49–50
in overly long sentences, 63, 69, 136
as used with vague *-ing* words, 32, 36, 134

and
correcting wordiness with, 75
as used to join subjects, 102, 141
in overly long sentences, 62–63, 68, 136
in wordy constructions, 82

answer key, 110–123

antecedents
agreement of, with pronouns, 106–109, 132–133
defined, 106, 124

apostrophes
correct use of, 90–93, 138–139
defined, 124

as
as used with misplaced modifiers, 50–51

as well as
  correcting wordiness with, 75
  in wordy constructions, 82

B

be, to
  nominalizations and, 24, 25
  passive voice and, 8, 11, 12, 14,
    16, 132–133
  as weak verb, 39, 40, 42, 43,
    44, 134
  in wordy constructions, 72, 74,
    77–80, 85, 87, 136

because
  in overly long sentences,
    63, 69, 136

before
  as used with misplaced
    modifiers, 49–50
  in overly long sentences,
    63, 69, 136
  as used with vague *-ing* words,
    32, 36, 134

but
  in overly long sentences,
    62–63, 68, 136

by
  as used with misplaced
    modifiers, 49–50
  passive voice and, 8, 11, 12, 13,
    16, 132–133
  as used with vague *-ing* words,
    32, 36, 134

C

can
  using, to correct wordiness, 78

clarity, 1, 2–4
 -ing words and, 30–31
  See also sentences, clear;
    subjects, clear; vagueness;
    verbs, clear

clauses
  defined, 125
  as misplaced modifiers, 51–53
  as modifiers, 103
  between subject and verb,
    102–103

clichés, 93–94, 138–139
  defined, 125

colons, 125

commas
  defined, 125
  in overly long sentences,
    62, 63, 64, 65
  as signals of misplaced
    modifiers, 49, 54, 57

comparisons, 98–102, 140–141

complete sentences, 125

compounds, hyphenated,
  96–98, 126

concision
  See wordiness

conjunctions
  run-on sentences and, 65
  See also and; but; or

consistency in pronoun use, 107

contractions
  apostrophes in, 91, 125, 138–139

countable nouns, 101, 125

D

dashes, em
  defined, 126

hyphens, confusing with, 98, 138
in overly long sentences,
64–65, 69, 136
deceit
indicating, with quotation
marks, 105–106, 137
despite the fact that
in wordy constructions, 75
dialogue
indicating, with quotation
marks, 105
different
as used to signal
comparisons, 99
do, to
nominalizations and, 24, 25
as weak verb, 32, 41, 44, 134
in wordy constructions, 80
drafts
wordiness in, 84
due to
as used with misplaced
modifiers, 49–50
as used with vague -ing words,
32, 36, 134

E
each and every
in wordy constructions, 76
editing
after drafting, 6, 71, 80
em dashes
defined, 126
hyphens, confusing with,
98, 138
in overly long sentences,
64–65, 69, 136

emphasis
incorrect use of quotation marks
to indicate, 105–106, 136
even though
in wordy constructions, 75
everybody
as singular indefinite
pronoun, 108
everyone
as singular indefinite
pronoun, 108
exclamation points, 126

F
fact that, the
in wordy constructions, 75
female
correct use of, as adjective,
109, 132–133
fewer vs. less, 100–101
fragments, 126

G
gender
of antecedents and singular
pronouns, 107
get, to
as weak verb, 39, 41, 44, 134
give ... the ability to
in wordy constructions, 80
go, to
as weak verb, 39, 41, 44, 134
grammar, 1–3
grammar-checking software
using, to spot wordy
sentences, 68

H

have the capability of
in wordy constructions, 81
have the effect of
in wordy constructions, 81
have, to
as weak verb, 39, 41, 44, 134
in wordy constructions, 80
he or she
referring back to a singular
antecedent, 108
homophones, 94–95, 140–141
however
correcting an overly long
sentence with, 63
hyphenated compounds,
96–98, 126, 138
hyphens
correct use of, 95–98, 138–139
defined, 126

I

ideas
too many, in a sentence,
61, 66–67
if
as used with misplaced
modifiers, 49–50
in overly long sentences,
63, 69, 136
as used with vague -*ing* words,
32, 36, 134
in a … manner
in wordy constructions, 76
in addition
correcting an overly long
sentence with, 63

in wordy constructions, 82
in spite of
in wordy constructions, 75
incomplete sentences, 126
indefinite pronouns, 108, 126
information
repeating, 72, 81–82
too much, in a sentence,
63, 66–67
-*ing* **words**
as misplaced modifiers, 49
as nominalizations, 22
vague, 27, 28–37, 131, 134–135
(*see also* vague -*ing* words)
instead of
as used with misplaced
modifiers, 49–50
as used with vague -*ing* words,
32, 36, 134
it
as used with misplaced
modifiers, 51
weak verbs and, 41, 44, 104, 134
in wordy constructions, 78
it is … that
in wordy constructions, 78
italics
using, to indicate emphasis,
106, 137
it's vs. its, 90–91, 92–93, 138

L

less
as used with adverbs and
adjectives, 100
fewer vs., 100–101
as used to signal comparisons, 99

like
as used with misplaced
modifiers, 50–51
as used to signal comparisons, 98

-ly
adding, to adjectives to make
adverbs, 76
adverbs ending in, incorrectly
using hyphens after, 98, 138

M

main verbs, 126.
See also verbs
make, to
as weak verb, 39, 41, 44, 134
in wordy constructions, 80
misplaced modifiers, 32, 45,
46–59, 134–135
beginning a sentence, 48–51
breaking up a sentence to
correct, 54–55
causes of, common, 53–56
defined, 126
detecting, 48–53
at the end of a sentence,
51–53
in the middle of a sentence,
51–53
after the verb, 56
modifiers
clauses as, 103
defined, 46, 48, 127
misplaced, 32, 45, 46–59, 126,
134–135 (*see also* misplaced
modifiers)
more
as used to signal comparisons, 99

mystery writers
vague language and, 35

N

nominalizations, 17, 18–27,
127, 132–133
acceptable use of, 25
clues signaling, 19, 21
correcting, 20–22
defined, 20–21, 127
passive voice with, 24
reasons to avoid, 22–25
wordiness and, 17, 20, 24–25,
74, 79, 83, 85
not only ... but also
in wordy constructions, 75
nouns
countable, 101, 125
defined, 106, 127
empty (*see* nominalizations)
hyphenating descriptive
compounds after,
97, 138–139
modifiers describing, 46, 55
nominalizations, 17, 18–27,
127, 132–133
plural, incorrect use of apostrophes in, 90, 93, 138
uncountable, 101, 130
vague, 104

O

objects, 10, 15, 16
in active sentences, 10, 124
in complete sentences, 125
defined, 127
passive voice and, 10, 15, 16

occur, to
 as weak verb, 39, 41, 134
of
 in nominalizations, 21, 132–133
on a ... basis
 in wordy constructions, 76
one
 as singular indefinite
  pronoun, 108
or
 as used to join subjects, 102
overly long sentences, 1, 59,
  60–71, 136–137
 clues signaling, 61, 62–66, 68
 correcting, 62–66
 reasons to avoid, 68

P

parallel sentences, 127
parentheses
 defined, 127
 in overly long sentences,
  64–65, 69, 136
 participles, past, 8, 11, 12, 16,
  50, 128, 132–133
 defined, 8, 11, 128
 misplaced modifiers and, 50
 See also verbs
passive sentences
 defined, 127
 See also passive voice
passive voice, 3, 4, 8–17,
  50, 132–133
 acceptable use of, 15, 16
 clues signaling, 8, 11
 correcting, 11–14
 defined, 10–11, 128

 eliminating all uses of, 15, 16
 formation of, 10–11
 -ing words and, 30
 nominalizations with, 24
 reasons to avoid, 13–15
 weak verbs and, 14
 wordiness and, 14, 74, 79, 83,
  85, 136
past participles
 defined, 8, 11, 128
 misplaced modifiers and, 50
 passive voice and, 8, 11, 12, 16,
  132–133
past-tense verbs, 8, 11, 128
 See also past participles; verbs
periods, 128
phrases
 defined, 128
 as misplaced modifiers, 51–53
 as modifiers, 48
 prepositional, 55, 128
 wordy, 72, 75–76
phrasing
 clear, 3 (*see also* clarity; sentences, clear; subjects, clear;
  vagueness; verbs, clear)
 concise (*see* wordiness)
 passive (*see* passive voice)
 vague, 1, 4 (*see also*
  vagueness)
plural
 defined, 128
 nouns, incorrect use of
  apostrophes in, 90, 93, 138
 pronouns, incorrect use of to
  refer back to singular antecedents, 106–108, 132

pompous language, 1, 42, 44, 101, 102, 105
possessives
apostrophes in, 91–92, 138–139
defined, 128
practicing good writing, 4–5, 6, 80
See also editing; rewriting
predicates, 126
See also verbs
prepositional phrases
defined, 128
misplaced modifiers and, 55
prepositions, 128
See also prepositional phrases
present-tense verbs, 129
See also verbs
pronoun-antecedent agreement, 106–109, 129, 132–133
pronouns
agreement of, with antecedents, 106–109, 132–133
in comparisons, 99
consistency in, 107
correct, after *than*, 101–102
defined, 106, 129
indefinite, 108, 126
plural, incorrectly referring back to a singular antecedent, 107
punctuation, 1
in overly long sentences, 61–66, 69
See also individual punctuation marks

Q

question marks, 129
quotation marks
correct use of, 105–106, 136–137
defined, 129
quotations, 105

R

reason that ... is because, the
in wordy constructions, 78, 136
repetition
of information in a sentence, 72, 81–82, 84, 85, 136
of synonymous words or phrases in a sentence, 82, 84, 85
of words in a sentence, 105
revision
See editing; rewriting
rewriting, 5–6, 71, 80
waiting a while before, 5, 82
run-on sentences, 65–66, 129

S

sarcasm
indicating, with quotation marks, 105–106, 137
semicolons, 129–130
sentence structure, 1
defined, 130
passive (*see* passive voice)
repetitive, 34
varying, 14, 23, 34
sentences
active, 14, 124
breaking up overly long, 54–55, 62–66, 67, 69, 104

clear, 3, 20, 30 *(see also* clarity;
    subjects, clear; vagueness;
    verbs, clear)
    complete, 125
    incomplete, 126
    overly long, 1, 59, 60–71,
        136–137 *(see also* overly long
        sentences)
    parallel, 127
    passive, 3, 4, 127 *(see also*
        passive voice)
    rewriting, 6
    run-on, 65–66, 129
    unparallel, 130
    vague, 1, 4, 20 *(see also*
        vagueness)
    varying, 14, 23, 34, 42, 68
serve to
    in wordy constructions, 81
similar
    as used to signal comparisons, 99
since
    as used with misplaced
        modifiers, 49–50
    in overly long sentences,
        63, 69, 136
    as used with vague *-ing* words,
        32, 36, 134
singular
    defined, 130
so
    in overly long sentences,
        63, 69, 136
somebody
    as singular indefinite
        pronoun, 108
sound-alike words, 94–95, 140–141

speech
    writing resembling, 3
spell-checking software
    sound-alike words and, 94
structure, sentence
    See sentence structure
subjects, 10, 15, 16
    in active sentences, 10, 124
    agreeing with verbs, 102–104,
        130, 140–141
    ambiguous, 33–34
    and joining, 102
    clear, 1, 10, 13, 27, 28, 30–31,
        32–35, 36, 37 *(see also* clar-
        ity; sentences, clear; vague-
        ness; verbs, clear)
    in complete sentences, 125
    defined, 130
    nominalizations and, 22–23, 27
    omitting, *-ing* words and,
        30–31, 32–34
    omitting, nominalizations and,
        22–23, 25
    omitting, passive voice and,
        13, 15
    or joining, 102
    passive voice and, 10, 13,
        15, 16
    plural, 102
    singular, 102
    vague, 17
    verbs placed far from, 67–68,
        102–104
    you as, 13–14, 23, 34
subject-verb agreement,
        102–104, 130, 140–141

T

than
in comparisons, 98, 99,
101–102
using correct pronoun after,
101–102

that
implied but omitted, 52–53
as used with misplaced
modifiers, 51–53, 134
omitted but implied, 52–53
weak verbs and, 41, 44
in wordy constructions,
77, 78, 79, 85

that is ... that
in wordy constructions,
78, 136

their
incorrectly referring back to a
singular antecedent, 107
they're vs., 91, 92

them
incorrectly referring back to a
singular antecedent, 107

then
incorrect use of, in comparisons, 100

there
as used with misplaced
modifiers, 51
weak verbs and, 41, 44,
134, 104
in wordy constructions, 77

there is ... that
in wordy constructions, 77

there is ... who
in wordy constructions, 77

they
incorrectly referring back to
a singular antecedent, 107

they're vs. their, 91, 92

this
weak verbs and, 41, 44,
104, 134
in wordy constructions,
77, 78

this is ... that
in wordy constructions, 78

those
in comparisons, 99

though
as used with misplaced
modifiers, 49–50
in overly long sentences,
63, 69, 136
as used with vague -*ing* words,
32, 36, 134

through
as used with misplaced
modifiers, 49–50
as used with vague -*ing* words,
32, 36, 134

-tion
in nominalizations, 22

tough
as used with vague -*ing* words,
32, 36

transitions
smooth, 67, 69, 137

U

uncountable nouns,
101, 130

underlining, 4

unlike

as used with misplaced
modifiers, 50–51

as used to signal comparisons, 98

unparallel sentences, 130

upon

as used with misplaced
modifiers, 49–50

as used with vague *-ing* words,
32, 36, 134

use, to

as weak verb, 39, 41, 44, 134

V

vague *-ing* words, 27, 28–37,
134–135

acceptable use of, 35

clues signaling, 28, 32

correcting, 30–32

defined, 30, 131

reasons to avoid, 32–35

vagueness, 1, 3, 4, 104

nominalizations and, 20

passive voice and, 10

wordiness and, 83–84

See also -ing words, vague;
passive voice

verbs

active, 1, 10

adding, to determine correct
pronoun after *than*, 102

agreeing with subjects, 102–
104, 130, 140–141

clear, 27, 33, 34–35, 37, 40, 42,
44, 135

in complete sentences, 125

creating nouns from, 20, 21, 26

defined, 131

forming, from nominalizations,
20–21, 26, 133

main, 126

misplaced modifiers after, 56

past participles, 8, 11, 12, 16,
132–133

past-tense, 128

present-tense, 129

strong, 24, 27, 40

subjects placed far from,
67–68, 102–104

varying, 42

weak, 14, 17, 24, 34–35, 38–45,
79, 81, 83, 104, 131, 134–135
(*see also* weak verbs)

voice

active (*see* active voice)

passive (*see* passive voice)

W

weak verbs, 14, 17, 24,
34–35, 38–45, 79, 81, 83,
104, 134–135

acceptable use of, 43–44

clues signaling, 39, 40–42, 44

correcting, 40–42, 44

defined, 40–42, 131

reasons to avoid, 42–43

when

in overly long sentences,
63, 69, 136

as used with vague *-ing* words,
32, 36, 134

whereas

as used with misplaced
modifiers, 49–50

as used with vague *-ing*
words, 32, 36, 134
which
in overly long sentences,
63, 69, 136
while
as used with misplaced
modifiers, 49–50
as used with vague *-ing* words,
32, 36, 134
who
implied but omitted, 52–53
as used with misplaced
modifiers, 52–53, 134
omitted but implied, 52–53
in overly long sentences,
63, 69, 136
who's vs. whose, 91, 92
woman
incorrect use of, as adjective,
109, 132–133
wordiness, 1, 72–87, 104,
136–137

acceptable, 84
causes of, 74, 81
clues signaling, 72, 74–82
correcting, 74–82
detecting, 72, 74–82
nominalizations and, 17, 20,
24–25, 74, 79, 83, 85
passive voice and, 10, 14, 74,
79, 83, 85, 136
reasons to avoid, 82–84
vagueness and, 83–84
weak verbs and, 43
words, sound-alike, 94–95,
140–141
writing
practicing, 4–5, 6
writing coach, 5

Y

you
as subject, 13–14, 23, 34
your vs. you're, 91, 92

ACKNOWLEDGMENTS

To my parents, Bart and Nancy Mills: Thank you for passing on your love of reading and writing, and many thanks for supporting me in everything I've done. No one could ask for better parental units.

To all the other writers in my family—A.P. Mills, Jeff Mills, Betty Mills, and Kevin Mills: You have inspired me.

To my past writing teachers, especially those at Cornell University: Thanks for making me write all those essays. I'd also like to acknowledge my Freshman Seminar teachers, who taught me about nominalizations and other nasty writing habits.

To all my copyediting clients, past and present: Thanks for letting me polish your prose. Don't read this book too closely, or you might not need me anymore!

To Meredith Brittain, Mark Eversman, Dave Tate, and Wendy McCord: Many thanks for all your input on the manuscript. Your suggestions and comments improved the book.

To my husband, Tom Trenga: Thanks for all the chocolates that have mysteriously materialized from your coat pockets over the years. Thanks also for your invaluable input as I worked on the book.

To the staff at F+W Publications: Many thanks to all who worked on the book. I'd especially like to thank Jane Friedman, who took on the project. I've enjoyed working with you.

ABOUT THE AUTHOR

Bonnie Trenga is a professional copyeditor and proofreader, and the author of *Off-the-Wall Skits With Phrasal Verbs*. She lives in Phoenix, Arizona. If you'd like to contact her, send an e-mail to curiouscase@hotmail.com.